Praise for *Energize*

'Energy is one of those things we all want more of but few have figured out how to find. And even fewer have figured out how to channel it even when they have found it. Simon's book is exactly what we need in this moment. With so many pulls and strains and stresses, he offers simple steps for every one of us to indeed energize!' Simon Sinek, optimist and *New York Times* bestselling author of *Start With Why*

'Learning how to manage your energy changes your life. Don't just read this book, do it!' Marie Forleo, author of the number one *New York Times* bestseller *Everything is Figureoutable*

'Thoughtfully written and incredibly researched, *Energize* will change the way you view energy in and around you. Simon provides practical advice to help you achieve your full potential in every area of your life. Exceptional!' Dr Marshall Goldsmith, Thinkers50 number one executive coach and *New York Times* bestselling author of *Triggers*

'This is not a one-time-read kind of book. This is a book to be absorbed, notes taken, reflected on and returned to again and again. Simon has packed so many takeaways into these pages you should be ordering it on Deliveroo. I loved it!' Andrea McLean, CEO and co-founder of This Girl Is On Fire and number one *Sunday Times* bestselling author

'If you want to make progress towards a legacy you can be proud of, read this transformative book. *Energize* shows you how to awaken your greatest sources of energy, rewire your mental blueprint so your mind is working for you and not against you, and protect your ability to focus on what matters most' Dorie Clark, *Wall Street Journal* bestselling author of *The Long Game* and executive education professor at Duke University Fuqua School of Business

'What a fantastic book! Simon is here to help us all find clarity and meaning in our lives' Adrienne Herbert, podcast host and author of *Power Hour*

'A must-read book that will inspire you to live a better story and awaken your imagination to what is truly possible' Keith Ferrazzi, number one *New York Times* bestselling author of *Never Eat Alone*

'Energy is life force; it is the magnet that attracts, repels and propels us forwards. *Energize* is your new battery pack for navigating the many personal, professional and global changes we are all facing. Simon Alexander Ong writes with clarity and grace on how to "perform effortless acts of alchemy" by harnessing this most vital resource' Jenny Blake, author of *Pivot*

'A game-changing book that will supercharge your life!' Bev James, *Sunday Times* bestselling author of *Do It! or Ditch It*

'Simon teaches you how to make the singular most pivotal investment of your life: the investment in your own energy' Patrick Drake, co-founder and former head chef of HelloFresh UK

'Simon is a force for positive personal change. Energy is contagious and this book teaches you how to boost yours and use it on the things that matter most' Zanna van Dijk, co-founder of Stay Wild and Forbes 30 Under 30 entrepreneur

'I believe that positive energy equals good business. Simon emanates this when he is addressing audiences of founders who bounce their positivity right back at him! This book will be a valuable guide to anyone looking to follow their own path and build energy levels through becoming their own boss' Emma Jones MBE, founder of Enterprise Nation

ABOUT THE AUTHOR

Simon Alexander Ong is a personal development entrepreneur, coach and public speaker. His clients are from all walks of life but they share one trait: they all believe that the greatest investment you can make is in yourself. His work has seen him invited on to Sky News, BBC Radio London and LBC Radio to be interviewed, and in 2018, Barclays UK featured him in a nationwide campaign asking him questions on how families can embrace better lifestyle habits. His insights have featured in *HuffPost*, *Forbes* and the *Guardian*. Simon regularly speaks for organizations and keynotes public events and conferences, including for the Peter Jones Foundation, the World Business and Executive Coach Summit and the London School of Economics. Simon is of Chinese origin and is based in London with his wife, Laurie, and daughter, Sienna.

Energize

Make the Most of Every Moment

Simon Alexander Ong

BUSINESS

PENGUIN BUSINESS

UK | USA | Canada | Ireland | Australia
India | New Zealand | South Africa

Penguin Business is part of the Penguin Random House group of companies
whose addresses can be found at global.penguinrandomhouse.com.

First published 2022

002

Copyright © Simon Alexander Ong, 2022

The moral right of the author has been asserted

'Worst Day Ever?' by copyright © Chanie Gorkin published by © poetrynation.com, 2017.

Letter to Ruth Bader Ginsburg written by Martin Ginsburg, 2010.
Reproduced by permission of Jim and Jane Ginsburg, the children of Martin and Ruth.

Annual letter to Amazon shareholders written by Jeff Bezos, 2015.
Published by © sec.gov, Exhibit 99.1.

Every effort has been made to trace or contact all copyright holders.
The publisher will be pleased to make good any omissions or rectify any mistakes
brought to their attention at the earliest opportunity.

Set in 13.5/16 pt Garamond MT Std
Typeset by Jouve (UK), Milton Keynes
Printed and bound in Great Britain by Clays Ltd, Elcograf S.p.A.

The authorized representative in the EEA is Penguin Random House Ireland,
Morrison Chambers, 32 Nassau Street, Dublin D02 YH68

A CIP catalogue record for this book is available from the British Library

ISBN: 978–0–241–50275–4

Follow us on LinkedIn: https://www.linkedin.com/company/penguin-connect/

www.greenpenguin.co.uk

MIX
Paper from
responsible sources
FSC® C018179
www.fsc.org

Penguin Random House is committed to a
sustainable future for our business, our readers
and our planet. This book is made from Forest
Stewardship Council® certified paper.

To my wife, Laurie.

I am grateful for the energetic partnership
that we have developed since the first day we met,
and for how you always inspire me to be a
better husband, father and human.

Contents

CONTENTS

Introduction:
Transform Your Energy, Transform Your Life

'If you want to find the secrets of the universe, think in terms of energy, frequency and vibration.'

NIKOLA TESLA

In yoga, they call it 'prana' and every physical manifestation of life is considered to be infused with it. In Maori culture, they call it 'mana'. In my Chinese culture, they call it 'chi' or 'qi', and in the field of traditional Chinese medicine it's considered to be the ultimate measure of our vitality. Whatever we choose to call it, we're all referencing the same thing: energy.

Energy is this universal language that communicates without words yet is still understood and felt by all – it knows when you're walking down the wrong path, when you're in a toxic relationship or when you're betraying your core values. And while it's invisible, like the Force in *Star Wars*, it speaks what our words so often struggle to convey through emotion; after all, emotions are nothing more than energy in motion.

There are people – let's call them 'energizers' – who lift you up and put you in the best of moods, and others – let's call them 'drainers' – who hoover up every drop of energy you have and leave you exhausted.

Energy is contagious.

It can spread rapidly to infect all areas of your life and those that come into close contact with you, regardless of whether the quality of that energy is positive or negative. It has the potential to create ripples of inspiration or tidal waves of chaos. Take a moment to reflect on the following: what impact does your energy have on those around you?

Think of energy as a form of power that we need to live and to thrive.

When feeling energized, we become the chief architect of our future and there's nothing that we feel we can't overcome. We see ourselves as unstoppable, and this activates our ability to perform effortless acts of alchemy – turning the invisible into the visible and the impossible into the possible. Once we understand how to awaken, nurture and protect this energetic force, it will breathe life into what we feel it is possible to accomplish during our time here on earth.

When we lack energy, we make poor decisions, easily get frustrated over the smallest of things and operate significantly below our potential. Everything feels like a chore and a never-ending struggle. While this isn't an ideal scenario, it's the unfortunate reality for so many of us.

As a result of our modern work culture, we're feeling more exhausted and working harder than ever, with little time to recharge. We seem to have more distractions and less energy. Our brains are tired from staring into screens all day. Without the awareness of how to use our energy efficiently, we allow it to slip away. And this places a barrier on our ability to thrive and enjoy life.

When it comes to productivity, energy really is everything. Without it, you can't get much done. Without it, you lack focus and discipline. Without it, a better life will remain just a distant dream. Your energy levels determine your state, who you attract into your life and how you do what you do. If you are to take advantage of the opportunities that arise in life, you must have the energy to do so.

Neuroscientist Dr Joe Dispenza wrote, 'The only way we can change our lives is to change our energy – to change the electromagnetic field we are constantly broadcasting. In other words, to change our state of being, we have to change how we think and how we feel.' This ability to master your energy is key to self-mastery – it's a powerful force and the better you are at managing it, the greater the impact on the way you live and work.

It's a truth that the world's most successful people understand. They may not be the strongest or the fastest, but they are the best when it comes to staying energized; they know that if you're always feeling exhausted, you can't possibly show up each day as your best self and achieve your most audacious goals. In fact, the bigger and bolder the goal, the more energy you will need.

Your focus must therefore shift from time management to energy management. Because no matter how well you manage your time, if you don't have the energy to follow through with what you have scheduled, you won't make much progress and the quality of what you do manage to get done will suffer. When you're time rich but energy poor, it's hard to do anything productive. When you're energized, however, you're able to accomplish much more, even when time may often be working against you. Throughout this book, you'll understand how to monitor and track your energy in the same way you already try to manage your time.

Learning how to manage this personal energy of yours means that you will possess the power to transform how you experience your life. To live in energetic flow is to be connected to your true self with a focus on living a life of purpose and meaning. It's an essential skill to master if you are serious about realizing your potential, because your best work can only flow from concentrating your attention on the things that matter to you.

It's why some people exhibit magnetic charisma simply through the incredible energy of their presence. This is what people refer to when they say that energy introduces you before you even speak, because energy from one person sparks energy in another. When you demonstrate the characteristics and qualities of an energizer, you don't just positively lift the mood of every room you're in, you experience improvement in your social life, your career, your relationships and family life.

In this book, you'll learn everything you need to know to begin injecting energy into every area of your life. This personal energy plan that you're holding in your hands will equip you with the wisdom required to awaken your power, rewire your energetic state, protect your personal energy and supercharge your impact. Put simply – by managing your energy more effectively and efficiently, it will help you get closer to achieving your goals in life.

Since learning how to master and transform my energy, I have seen extraordinary things happen in my life:

- I found the courage to leave behind an unful-
filling corporate career and enter the world of

entrepreneurship as a coach. Since then, I have helped hundreds of clients go from energy poverty to energy abundance. These have included the likes of startup entrepreneurs, Michelin Star chefs, C-Suite executives, TV presenters, fund managers and government officials.

- I was named Life Coach of the Year at the International Coaching Awards and received a national award by Junior Chamber International (an international non-profit organization focused on encouraging young people to become active citizens and leaders within their communities), for the positive impact of my work on the lives of others.

- I grew from someone who was extremely shy and introverted to someone who has been invited to speak at some of the planet's most successful companies, to partner with globally recognized brands such as Barclays and Unilever on national and regional campaigns, and to share my insights on TV and radio, including Sky News and the BBC.

- I have also had the opportunity to speak in front of audiences across the world at conferences held in America, Australia, Belgium, Bulgaria, Estonia, Indonesia and the UK.

- I am blessed to be working with an incredible publishing team at Penguin Random House, who have helped me to share my thoughts and insights with you in this book.

Most importantly, though, the insights and lessons contained in this book have helped me become the most energized that I have ever felt – from a physical, mental and spiritual perspective. In fact, I can promise you this: once you experience what it's truly like to lead a supercharged life, you will never want to go back to the way you felt before.

If you commit to applying the wisdom that will be shared in the following pages, you too will be well on your way to unlocking your most energetic self and, in the process, discovering that you are far greater than you ever imagined.

This book may have found its way into your hands because you're fed up with always feeling exhausted, or you're hearing a voice from within constantly whispering, 'You are capable of more. You are destined for something greater than where you currently are. The world hasn't seen the best of what you have to offer yet.'

If this is you, then I can relate, because I was in exactly the same position before undergoing a personal metamorphosis. Those feelings of discomfort and frustration were life demanding a better version of myself start showing up. And to be the change that I wanted to see, I had to be a better steward of my energy, such that mind and body could be firing on all cylinders.

Taking action today to address your physical, mental, emotional and spiritual energy will contribute not only to a longer life but to one rich in feelings of happiness, joy and fulfilment. And as you start to become more conscious of your energy and embrace this life force, you will quickly discover yourself achieving more of that potential that we were all born with. Who wouldn't want that?

The opposite of a default future is a consciously created life, and to achieve this requires energy. So, if you're ready to begin on the path to feeling energized and supercharged, let's get started . . .

PART 1

Awaken Your Power

1
Invest in
Your Health

The moment I collapsed in the bath with a splitting headache, smelling of alcohol and still fully dressed in my suit at 3.30 a.m., I knew that something had to change.

No more indecision and waiting for things to happen. I was burning out fast, nosediving head first into a chaotic downward spiral that meant, if I didn't put the brakes on to address it, I would stand to lose my health, my girlfriend and any hope for a better future.

I wasn't sure how long I had been lying there, but given how damp my socks were, I assumed it must've been longer than just a few minutes. As I struggled to open my eyes, which was made worse by the fact that my contact lenses had now been on for well over twenty hours, I saw my girlfriend Laurie kneeling on the floor beside me in tears.

A few hours earlier I had dropped her a quick call to say that I would be taking the last train home, before descending into an underground nightclub in London for a client event. The drinks were free-flowing, the music was loud and the entertainment was extravagant. As the night went on my phone lost reception, and as my body became flooded with alcohol, I lost all perception of time.

Concerned about my welfare and worried that I should've already been home, Laurie was unable to get through to me. I don't know how I did it, but after stumbling out of the club around 2 a.m., I was able to somehow hail a taxi to get me home.

As Laurie voiced her concerns and reminded me that I had to be back in the office for 7 a.m., the only words I could slur in response were, 'I'm fine.' The harsh truth, however, was that I was far from fine. I felt exhausted, directionless and completely lost. Waking up each morning to commute into work was a struggle, and I would find myself easily jumping into activities that helped me to escape the reality I was living – binge-watching an entire TV series over the weekend, partying into the early hours of the next day and gambling my money away in the hope that I could buy myself out of the hole I was in.

I was working in the financial services industry at the worst possible time. The global financial crisis was bringing econ- omies across the world to their knees, and having managed to leave Lehman Brothers just before its collapse in Septem- ber 2008, I was now working for a company that was costing me my health. The hours were long and punishing, with little in the way of career development. I was surviving off takeaways and catching up with sleep during my commute to and from work. And as one of just a handful of junior members on the team, I was regularly shouted at by my seniors.

I remember walking into the office one morning to discover that one of my colleagues hadn't shown up. His name was Daniel and he was a hardworking guy who had dreams of making it big in the industry. However, there was a limit to what he could take. Senior management failed to get hold of him, and as I began to fear the worst, I received a text message that simply said, 'Tell them I'm not coming back to the office. Ever.' While many laughed at what had happened that day, I took it as a sign; a sign that maybe this industry wasn't meant for me.

A couple of days later, when I was in a more sober state, I found the courage to share the truth with Laurie. Growing up, I was always told to 'man up', that 'boys don't cry' and not to 'act like a girl'. It's no wonder that I found it difficult to express my feelings and emotions in front of someone else. I was afraid of being judged and so I tried to deal with everything on my own by putting on a brave face, so as to not allow others to see what was really happening. However, as Brené Brown wrote in her book *The Gifts of Imperfection*, 'Only when we are brave enough to explore the darkness will we discover the infinite power of our light.'

During our conversation, Laurie said, 'It feels like you've lost that spark and I don't think you're going to rediscover it at the place you're at. I'm looking at you and can't help but think how much this job is killing your health and squeezing you dry of any energy you have.'

She was right – there was no fuel left in the tank.

I had arrived at this place where I no longer wanted what I once thought I did, and where the pain of continuing as things were was now outweighing the pain of radical change. I knew that whatever I wasn't changing, I was choosing. And I didn't like what I was choosing at all. If what I was currently doing was going to cost me my health, then it really wasn't worth staying. There are pivotal moments in our lives that have the power to thrust us into an entirely new story from which there is no return, and this was going to be one of them.

That same evening, I typed out a short resignation letter, handed it in the next morning with my heart racing because of the uncertainty that lay ahead, and got to work on awakening that fire of aliveness inside of me. And I knew exactly where I had to start from. It was the area of my life that had deteriorated the most: my health.

Stop treating your health as a side hustle

If I were to ask you what your energy levels are like right now, what would you say?

During our first meeting, many clients tell me how stressed they are, how tired they feel and how busy they always seem to be. Some have even shared how they lack the energy to engage with activities that they once enjoyed and how they get easily frustrated over the most trivial of things – something that has impacted the quality of their relationships with others.

If we take a look at the people around us, it's easy to observe just how common these feelings are. It's the result, in part, of the explosion and glorification of busyness. Our society is addicted to stress. It's no surprise that we're completely overwhelmed by the frenetic pace of modern life. We need to flip the narrative so that rather than being seen as a badge of honour or a status symbol, we must recognize these responses as the health warning that they are and change our behaviour before our energy reservoir sinks too low.

Investing in a healthier lifestyle is a wise strategy not just because it will contribute to a longer lifespan, but because it will also build your confidence, elevate your mood and unleash your creativity. While physical energy is just one element in your personal energy plan, it's the first you must address, because it provides you with the basic energy levels required to successfully navigate the demands that each day brings. It also has a positive impact on all other areas of your life, especially your mental health and ability to focus.

Neglecting it means that you risk carrying an energy deficit with you through lost sleep, skipped meals, an unhealthy diet or being glued to your chair in front of screens. Making changes here will result in your energy levels soaring to new heights and will make an immediate difference to the way you feel and perform.

Awareness about the detrimental effects of overwork on our health and productivity may have grown significantly, but there still seems to be a prevailing sense that taking care of our well-being is a luxury or something that we can address when time allows. Don't get me wrong. I believe that hard work is very important if you want to get far in life. But if you want to thrive and enjoy this rare gift of life, you must avoid focusing on only the grind and running yourself into the ground.

Health is so often cited as the first wealth for good reason: without it, you can't do much else. It's why the healthy person has many wishes while the sick have just one. If you plan on living a long life – one that is full of energy, excitement and adventure – this is where it begins. You must make your health a priority. Mountains simply cannot be climbed if you're always feeling exhausted because the energy that's required for you to go after what matters most to you will be non-existent.

This chapter focuses on what I consider to be the cornerstone habits of good health – habits that have provided me with the platform to transform my life for the better:

1. Sleep
2. Exercise
3. Diet

These are simple solutions. The most powerful often are, but because of their simplicity we tend to overlook them and overcomplicate matters. If you're serious about managing your energy in a sustainable way, however, they must form the core of your energy management strategy, because without them in place, you will always be short on energy. And you can't accomplish anything great if you're not feeling great from within first.

This ability to operate at a higher level of energy – driven by both your physical and mental capacity – sharpens your productivity and provides you with the quality fuel required to take action on all those things that you are telling yourself that you want to do.

Just as the strongest trees have deep and extensive root systems in the ground that they stand on, cultivating a solid foundation grounded in good health will give you the platform you need to accomplish extraordinary things in life. It will take you from sleepy to supercharged, because the energy you need to transform your future can only develop once you begin to take better care of yourself in the present.

Changing your lifestyle might just prove to be your first-class ticket to success and it's time you gave it the attention it deserves. If you don't, you will eventually be faced with no choice but to spend a lot of time dealing with illness. Choose wisely . . .

Sleep better, live better

Sleep specialist Dr Matthew Walker wrote in his book *Why We Sleep*: 'One of the biggest reasons that people don't get enough sleep is because they feel they have too much to do or because they are stressed about what they need to work on. So we're not getting enough work done because we're sleep deprived and we're not sleeping because we're not getting enough work done.'

Too many of us are stuck in this vicious cycle that Walker describes, and with the belief that there is a sleep crisis in our culture he goes on to add that, 'Most people equate losing sleep with having more time to enjoy the day or getting things done. Ironically, when they are sleep deprived, they enjoy the day less and are so unfocused that they are much slower in getting things done.'

Sleep, it seems, tends to be one of the first things we sacrifice, on the assumption that by doing so we will become more accomplished. But this couldn't be further from the truth, because when you begin a new day without sufficient rest and with low-quality sleep, your physical, mental and emotional energy suffer. And you end up relying on stimulants such as caffeine and energy drinks to get you through. It's like starting a race 100 metres behind your fellow competitors. You'll find yourself playing catch up all day because you're operating at a fraction of what you're capable of. Instead of being in control of your day, the day is in control of you.

During one client coaching session, it was clear just how much of an impact insufficient sleep can have on our levels of energy. Michael came to me as a high-achieving leader within the hospitality industry, with his fascinating journey well covered and documented by the press. Behind the scenes, however, he was struggling to make the progress he wanted in order to jump to the next level in his career. Our conversation went something like this as we started this particular session:

ME: Tell me a little more about what stopped you following through with what you said you were going to do?

MICHAEL: [*Sighs*] Honestly? Well, there has certainly been some procrastination – no doubt about it. The energy to do it just hasn't been there either. I mean, it should. My girlfriend is away for the next few weeks working on a client project and during this time I feel like I'll be more in control of how I use my time. There just seems to be no time to get everything I want to get done, done.

ME: You say that the energy to do it just hasn't been there. I'm noticing that your eyes are looking a little tired and you also seem a little frazzled. What has your sleep been like?

MICHAEL: I could definitely do with more. What would help is to better manage the distractions that have got the better of me recently. My phone has been the main culprit and even comes with me into the bedroom before I sleep. It's not healthy and it has been challenging trying to peel myself away from it and before I know it, the whole evening is gone. Last night wasn't too bad, though. Actually, I still didn't end up going to bed until the middle of the morning after I ended watching a few episodes of a new Netflix show that a friend recommended to me.

Today, Michael is usually in bed by 11 p.m., with his phone on flight mode until the next morning when he has finished eating breakfast with his girlfriend. Prior to going to bed, he now plans out his most important tasks for the next day and reads industry-related literature or books that will help him grow as a human and a leader for the people that he's responsible for. As this routine became the norm for him, he quickly discovered that he wasn't the only one to benefit from his ability to show up each day with more energy and focus. He shared that 'My girlfriend has noticed a difference. My team has noticed a difference. Even my business partner has noticed a difference in the way I show up to work each day. The energy I now have is incredible. It has given me the focus to launch an exciting new project that I had previously been stalling on and I can't wait to share more with you once the plans have been approved.'

As a coach, the turnaround that he experienced was beautiful to witness. More rested and waking each morning with more energy, addressing his sleep would prove to be the beginning of the domino effect in action – the process of one behaviour change leading to a change in other related areas of his life. He picked up cycling again, transformed his diet and schedules one day a week for a complete digital detox.

The reality is that our most productive days always begin with getting high-quality sleep, as it is this that sets the stage for better decisions, for waking up with greater energy and increased levels of emotional intelligence. Sleep is the foundation of our physical energy and contributes to our ability to live up to our potential by providing us with the fuel and focus that we need. We are like a battery, and sleep is how we get to recharge that battery.

How much is enough sleep?

Some will say that five or six hours will suffice. Others will say that you need a solid eight. While the true number may lie somewhere between the two, the best way to judge whether you need more is to reflect on this question: do you regularly feel tired and exhausted when you wake up in the morning? If the answer is yes, then it's a good sign that you must get more sleep.

For parents, a baby's first year can wreak havoc on even the best of sleep routines. It really makes them appreciate just how important sleep is. When babies get enough sleep, the world is fine and everything is great. When they don't, nothing is and chaos ensues. The same applies to you. While I understand that getting enough sleep is not always possible (note: I'm a parent myself), in many cases it's our own self-sabotaging behaviour that is the real challenge to overcome. It's the avoidable habits of not being able to detach ourselves from our digital devices, TV or work that are to blame. This behaviour – bedtime procrastination if you will – starves you of the energy you need to be at your best come tomorrow morning.

The American essayist and poet Ralph Waldo Emerson advised us to 'Finish each day before you begin the next, and interpose a solid wall of sleep between the two.' And the key to getting a solid wall of sleep is designing a sleep routine that heightens the quality of the sleep you get. The goal for us, here, is to make bedtime something to look forward to and the environment as conducive to sleep as possible. Because how well you sleep is determined by what you do before going to bed.

Here are three strategies to get you started on designing a routine that will help you sleep better and wake up full of energy:

1. The 3–2–1 rule

Three hours before bed, log off from all work-related activities and use this time to review your day and to plan the next day's priorities. Doing so will help you fall asleep significantly faster because you won't go to bed figuring out what to do tomorrow. Two hours before bed, say no to any more eating and use this time to wind down and get yourself in the right frame of mind for bed. One hour before bed, escort any digital devices out of the bedroom and use this time for relaxing activities such as reading, journalling, taking a warm bath, visualization or meditation. To accompany these, I tend to have calming instrumental music in the background, together with soft lighting.

2. Stop being a dayist

We are dayists when we discriminate between different days of the week, and overcoming this when it comes to having a regular sleep routine is important. Going to sleep and waking up at the same time each day, even on weekends, will dramatically improve the quality of your sleep. Whenever I have an irregular sleep routine, it takes me longer to fall asleep and my overall sleep quality ends up being poor.

3. Check into a hotel room every night

Whenever I ask people when they have experienced their best sleep, most tell me about a hotel or resort where they were a guest during their travels. It's understandable when you think about it – the relaxing environment that is clean and clutter-free, the quality of the bedding used and that feeling of fresh sheets. The environment of the rooms has been optimized for the purpose of quality sleep, and it's something we can also do to make our bedroom a more inviting place to be in the evening – like checking into your very own hotel room each night. Given that we spend around a third of our lives sleeping, it makes sense to invest in a better sleep environment.

My message to you here is not to underestimate the importance of sleep if you want to wake up full of energy. You can't outrun the consequences of insufficient rest forever. They will eventually catch up with you through an increase in almost every type of major health-related problem.

In fact, all the studies and literature I have read around this topic point to the same conclusion: the shorter your sleep, the shorter your life. As Dr Thomas Roth, Director of the Sleep Disorders and Research Center at Henry Ford Hospital in Detroit since 1978, put it: 'The number of people who can survive on five hours of sleep or less without impairment, and rounded to a whole number, is zero.' If you are getting by with just a couple of hours of sleep a night, then no productivity hack can help you. Make sure you are working with your body, not against it.

Exercise to energize

Dedicated. Determined. Disciplined.

These three words can be seen printed across all of Ernestine Shepherd's gym clothing and they make up the mantra that has energized her for over three decades. Early to rise each morning, she runs at least ten miles a day (around eighty miles a week) and her 5K time is under half an hour. Following her morning runs, she hits the gym for up to an hour, lifting weights at least four days a week. She is a model who holds two bodybuilding competition titles, has completed nine marathons, works as a personal trainer and is an author.

These accomplishments are all the more impressive once you learn that she is eighty-five years old and is already living well past the average life expectancy of women in the United States, where she resides.

In the many interviews that she has done about her extra-ordinary body transformation, she often says, 'If there is an anti-ageing pill, I would call it exercise.' She feels better today than she did when she was forty and radiates more energy than those who are decades younger than her. The energy that Shepherd feels is no surprise, and the benefits are clear to see. In fact, greater amounts of physical activity have been regu-larly associated with a lower risk of dying from cancer, and the more people move, the lower this risk.

Exercise is like our soldier in the war against ill health, nourishment for our personal energy and a vaccine that helps to level up our immune system.

At an age when many regard themselves to be 'old' and declining in terms of their physical capabilities, Shepherd's story is an inspiring example of age being just a number and that it's never too late to start. She believes that exercise should play an integral part in everyone's day, no matter your age, and demon-strates that age or physical ability must never be used as an excuse to skip out on getting your body moving. Because the more you move, the more energetic you feel.

Whenever I'm asked about how I seem to have consistently high levels of energy, I always mention my exercising habit that I begin each day with. It's an absolute non-negotiable because of the profound impact that it has had on my energy and, as a result, on other areas of my life: from eating better to consuming less alcohol, and to greater self-confidence and self-esteem. This is how I see it: an hour of exercise takes up less than 5% of your day but has the power to transform your future, and whenever I think about this, I always find an hour to show up and put in the reps. If your health is important enough to you, you will make time for it.

And it seems I'm far from alone on this. Some of the most successful people that I have read about and listened to credit exercise as playing an instrumental role in what they've been able to achieve. Co-founder and CEO of Facebook Mark Zuckerberg, for example, shared that 'Staying in shape is very important. Doing anything well requires energy, and you just have a lot more energy when you're fit.'

That feeling of euphoria that is so often felt after a session of exercise is driven by the release of endorphins that wake our body up from the inside. These endorphins make us happy, and being happy gives us energy. To illustrate the influence that exercise has on our energy, University of Georgia researchers published a study in the journal *Psychotherapy and Psychosomatics* in 2008 that found inactive people who normally complained about fatigue could experience an energy jump of up to 20% and a fall in fatigue of as much as 65% by simply participating in regular, low-intensity exercise.

When you think about it, the long-term effects of exercise on the mind and body are insane. Not only is it one of the best things you can do for your energy and mental wellbeing because of the endorphins that are released into your body, but it also makes you stronger and helps contribute to a longer life. It lifts your mood, clarifies your thinking and reminds you of just how incredible it feels to be alive. Bill Bowerman – co-founder of Nike – said that 'If you have a body, you are an athlete.' You're an athlete because, as humans, our bodies are designed to move, not to sit down all day and be slumped into a sedentary lifestyle.

However you choose to move your body, the key is that you should enjoy the activities you participate in. The gym doesn't always have to be the default option when you think about adopting a more active lifestyle.

Given her love of the outdoors, adventurer and endurance athlete Sophie Radcliffe didn't go to the gym for many years during her fitness journey. And as someone who describes herself as 'not a natural athlete', with no background in fitness, she wanted to find something that would motivate her to get fit. This led to her taking on her first challenge, which was an adventure race through the jungles of Borneo called the Kinabalu Challenge – a week-long race that involved mountain biking, trail running, kayaking, white-water rafting, jungle camp building, bartering in local markets and climbing to the summit of Mount Kinabalu.

This was followed by a triathlon event run by Eurostar that took place across three cities in one day – swim in Paris, bike in Brussels and run in London. Because she enjoyed the cycling element of the triathlon, Sophie went on to cycle from London to Paris in twenty-four hours and London to Amsterdam in forty-eight hours.

Since then, she has gone on to climb mountains, complete some of the world's toughest Ironman triathlons, captain a bike race from Los Angeles to Miami, and launch a not-for-profit youth empowerment initiative to help teenage girls develop the mindset and skills to live courageously. And in 2014 she became the only person in history to cycle across the eight Alpine countries (Slovenia, Austria, Germany, Liechtenstein, Switzerland, France, Italy and Monaco) and climb each of their highest mountains over a thirty-two-day period.

When I interviewed Radcliffe, she shared that her number one strategy for creating positive energy is exercise and that such an active lifestyle strengthened her self-belief and courage to ask for more in all areas of her life. And instead of exercising making her tired, she discovered that it flooded her with energy as her body rose up to meet the challenges she gave it. She noted that when she's not exercising, she's starving her mind and body of what it needs for her to feel great, adding, 'It's amazing to be living this lifestyle and inspiring others through my journey to get the most out of their lives. A lot of what we want is in other people's hands, such as our boss giving us a promotion. With physical challenges, however, I feel like I can achieve anything I set my mind to.'

You may not always feel like getting up and moving your body each day, but as Radcliffe pointed out during our conversation, you never regret it once you've finished; even if the activity you do is of low intensity. You come out feeling far more energetic than when you went in, and your body will ultimately thank you for it.

Here are three ways to help you get up, get moving and get energized:

1. Feel like a superhero

If you're only exercising in order to lose weight, get that six-pack or have bodybuilder arms, it's going to be very easy for you to give up the habit of regular exercise because these things are not happening overnight. Instead, ask yourself each morning, 'How good do I want to feel today?' and then focus on all the benefits that you will experience from getting your body moving. As Nelson Mandela wrote in his autobiography,

Long Walk to Freedom, 'I have always believed exercise is a key not only to physical health but to peace of mind.'

2. Design an exercise menu and select to fit your mood

My starters include swimming, long walks outside in nature, yoga, housework and app-based workouts, which I can do from anywhere in the world with an internet connection and little to no equipment. My main course options offer cycling, weight training, boxing and bootcamp classes. On some days, I'll settle for just a starter, while on other days I'll dive straight into the main course. And from time to time, I'll go for both a starter and a main. Keeping things varied keeps things exciting and interesting. What would you have on your exercise menu?

3. Gamify the experience

The process of gamification can heighten your engagement in an activity and motivate you to achieve more. In my cycling class, for example, there's a leaderboard at the front of the class that ranks participants on a variety of metrics. This sense of friendly competition (against yourself and others) and community in exercising as part of a group inspires you to improve each time you show up to class. Those who invest in a fitness tracker also find themselves moving on a more regular basis, and more inclined to take the stairs instead of the lift and to walk instead of drive.

More ideas
Here are a few more suggestions for how to make exercise more fun and something that you can look forward to. The

idea here is to get creative around making it a core part of your daily routine.

- Ditch the boardroom for the great outdoors by holding more regular walking meetings. It will give you the opportunity to unplug from your devices, breathe fresh air into your creativity and get your body moving. Movement, combined with a change in scenery, will energize your thinking.
- Take on a challenge with a partner or group of friends. This can include learning how to dance with your loved one, practising martial arts as a family or signing up as a group to run a marathon and raise money for charity in the process. The accountability built into this will help you show up and follow through.
- Liven up your routine with exergaming – a fitness trend that offers a physical twist to the traditional way of playing video games. Depending on the video game you are playing, you can select from a wide library of exercise options, all while overcoming a fire-breathing dragon, escaping from danger in a futuristic cityscape or competing against players living on another continent.

Upgrade the quality of your fuel

Arriving in England from Japan in 1996 to manage Arsenal football club, one of the key areas that Arsène Wenger was focused on changing for his players was their nutrition. During his time in Japan managing Nagoya Grampus, he observed that there was almost no obesity. He explained, 'I lived for two years in Japan and it was the best diet I ever had. Their diet is basically boiled vegetables, fish and rice. No fat, no sugar. You notice when you live there that there are no fat people. I think in England you eat too much sugar and meat and not enough vegetables.' The core of his philosophy was simple: eat too much sticky toffee pudding and you will play like one. In other words, if you want to perform at your best, then what you eat matters.

Wenger made a valid point with his observations. Since his remarks, obesity has risen to epidemic proportions globally, with at least 2.8 million people dying each year as a result, and has become one of the leading causes of preventable deaths. It causes thirteen types of cancer and in 2020, as the coronavirus pandemic spread rapidly across the world, a study by the University of North Carolina at Chapel Hill found that obesity increased the risk of coronavirus-related deaths by nearly 50%.

Sir Simon Stevens, former chief executive of NHS England, even warned that obesity has now become the new smoking. Changes to our food environment have resulted in our minds being constantly bombarded by and exposed to junk food and sugary drinks. From clever marketing to strategic placement of products, our willpower is being tested like never before.

Once Wenger started to apply his football philosophy, it didn't take long for Arsenal's players to become some of the fittest and leanest in the English Premier League. By 1998, he guided the club to its first championship title in seven years. They went on to also capture the FA Cup trophy, clinching their first such double since 1971. Manchester United's Gary Neville even labelled the class of '98 as the best English side he had faced during his career, saying, 'That 1998 Arsenal team had everything: pace, power, strength, great defenders, a good goalkeeper and good finishers. That was a complete team.' A couple of years later, in 2004, Arsenal won the title again without losing a single match – a feat that earned them the nickname 'Invincibles'.

What Wenger and his dietician demonstrated is that the food you consume must be something that serves you. It should provide you with all the nutrients that your body requires to stay healthy. Since one of our primary sources of energy comes from the food that we eat, we must be conscious and mindful of what we consume. Food is fuel, and the better the fuel, the better your body operates.

In her online article for *Precision Nutrition* entitled 'Mood Food: How to Fight Depression Naturally with Nutrition', Camille DePutter noted that '60 litres of blood are pumped into your brain every hour, providing oxygen, removing waste products and delivering nutrients. If that blood is nutrient-deficient, or carrying junk that doesn't belong, it's going to interfere with your brain's function – specifically its ability to create necessary neurotransmitters.' These neurotransmitters are chemical messengers required by the brain to help regulate many important functions such as our mood, ability to focus and sleep cycles. Without the right nutrients, our brain simply won't get what it needs, and DePutter notes that 'nutrient deficiencies often look like mental health problems'. Unhealthy foods, it seems, can affect our mental health and kill our energy.

When it comes to upgrading the quality of your fuel, one of the fastest ways to be in control of your eating and the impact that food has on your energy is the habit of meal planning – deciding in advance what you're going to eat. In addition to the obvious health benefits, it saves you time, money and an incredible amount of mental energy deciding what to shop for and cook each day. And when you have meals that fuel your body with the nutrition it needs planned and prepared in advance, you won't find your monkey brain marching you into a fast-food joint or filling in a takeaway order when hunger strikes.

Eating smarter in this way was a natural consequence of making daily exercise non-negotiable. I didn't want all that hard work that I was doing in order to feel energetic to be swiftly undone by a poor diet. At the beginning of each week, therefore, my wife and I sit down and plan out our family's meals for the week ahead. And instead of following extreme diet plans or trends that can often suck the joy out of eating, we prefer to follow a few fundamental principles that have helped us to maintain a high level of energy:

1. Become a waterholic

With 60% of our bodies comprised of water, drinking enough of the stuff is essential to feeling energized and mentally sharp. A lack of it, on the other hand, will result in periods of fatigue and low energy as our body struggles to function without enough water. It's why we always have a bottle of water within easy reach at home, in the office and when travelling.

2. Think inside the bento box

The bento box is a concept that has been used for centuries in Japan to control portion sizes and to carry delicious, nutritious food that is well balanced. It's an appreciation of how the way we fuel our bodies has a significant impact on our energy levels throughout the day. A bento box typically consists of food such as rice (40%), fish or meat (30%), vegetables and pickles (30%), separated into compartments and visually appealing in terms of colour combinations. The lesson that we can apply from thinking inside the bento box is to build our meals around the ideas of moderation, variety and balance, with a bias towards foods that provide our bodies with a natural source of energy. And the more colourful it looks, the better.

3. Go bananas

There's a good reason why bananas are often referred to as the perfect snack for athletes: they deliver an immediate and substantial boost of energy, as well as containing nutrients that lift your mood. In fact, a diet rich in fresh fruit will do wonders for your energy and is the reason we have replaced unhealthy, highly processed snacks in our home with a wide variety of fruit. There's a well-known proverb that says, 'An apple a day keeps the doctor away.' For me, I see it as, 'A generous bowl of fruit a day keeps the doctor away.'

What goes into your meal plan for the week will be personal to you, as we all have different energy requirements. When I interviewed Rhiannon Lambert, a leading Harley Street nutritionist and author of *Re-Nourish: A Simple Way to Eat Well*, she noted that our activity level dramatically alters what kind of nutrition we need. The requirement for those who exercise twice a day isn't going to be the same as for those who exercise just a couple of times a week. 'Fuelling your body with the right nutrients, prior to and during a long day of work,' she says, 'will give you the energy and strength you need to operate at your best. You also need to adapt your meals to your schedule by taking into account your daily energy requirements and in doing so, you'll start listening to your body. After all, the amount of energy we have determines what we do and the food we consume has a big role to play in this.'

Food must be something that serves you and provides you with the energy you need. You may think that this is an obvious point, but how often have you sabotaged your health with eating and drinking habits that you know are far from nourishing for your body? Overeating, indulging in heavily processed foods and drinking too much alcohol will affect more than just your weight. It will drain your energy and vitality.

2
Elevate Your Consciousness

'He who knows others is wise.
He who knows himself is enlightened.'

LAO TZU

At the age of nine, and barely able to speak English, Diana Chao's family relocated from one of the poorest provinces in China to Southern California, where she found herself in a predominantly white town. It was a culture shock. Not only was she growing up under the poverty line, but because her parents couldn't speak a word of English, they faced a mountain of difficulties when it came to healthcare and navigating life through the years that coincided with the 2007–8 global recession.

Determined not to fall behind her fellow students at school, Chao spent her free time reading in the library and listening to audio tapes to improve her English. A year later, remarkably, she had caught up with her class in English proficiency and was scoring perfect marks in grammar tests that left her teachers speechless.

By thirteen years old, she was working multiple jobs to bring in money for the family: everything from distributing free product samples at Costco, to being a janitor, a forklift driver at a local warehouse and a real-time translator. She was learning all the time, tapping into that energetic feeling of possibility that comes from developing new skills, and after teaching herself photography, coding and design she became a conceptual and fashion photographer for outlets such as *Vogue Italia* and Adobe.

Around the same time she was diagnosed with bipolar disorder and with uveitis, an eye disease that rendered her blind for weeks at a time whenever an episode struck. She spent high school in and out of hospital, the worst experience coming in February of her sophomore year when she was rushed to the emergency room. Struck with an extremely high fever, she fell into a coma and was put on life support as her senses of hearing, sight and taste abandoned her. This, together with the pressure of growing up in a poverty-stricken household, led her to attempt suicide multiple times.

Despite being introduced to Child Protective Services after scars were discovered across her entire body, it wasn't until her little brother caught her on the brink of death that she made a promise to herself that she had to find a way to heal, no matter what it took.

She had taken on the role of a parent to her brother and so, in a way, viewed him as a sort of son. So for him to see her in this terrible state forced her to make a resolution that no matter how dark her world got, she would not drag him down with her. The closeness of this sibling relationship equipped her with the energy to seek solutions to the challenges she was experiencing.

And this is when she turned to writing.

When I interviewed her for this book, she told me that 'It was writing that saved my life.' It became a mechanism for healing – a space to discover her worth, her voice and her purpose. 'Writing,' she shared, 'is humanity distilled into ink.'

Because the triggers and trauma often originated from those closest to her, she needed to talk – or at least feel like she was talking – to someone outside her current circle. Her writing therefore took the form of letters to strangers she had never met who were going through their own challenges – a fictional character from a novel that she had read, or someone in the real world. The process raised her awareness of how kind and empathetic she was to them but not to herself. By having this space to explore her thoughts and emotions, it helped her to connect more deeply with her soul.

Given the impact that writing had on her life, she began to reflect on how it could also help others to learn about themselves in the same way. The thought led her to start Letters to Strangers (L2S) in 2013 as a student club at high school, to help others tell their own stories by writing anonymous, heartfelt letters to share their vulnerabilities and offer support to those fighting through difficult times. Each is addressed in the same way: to and from a stranger.

Before she knew it, interest began to snowball and other schools were inspired to start a chapter of her club.

What began as a small high school club quickly became the largest youth-for-youth mental health non-profit on the planet, with 35,000+ in the L2S network in over twenty countries. In 2018, she became the youngest ever recipient of the Unilever Young Entrepreneurs Award; in 2019, she was named an *Oprah Magazine* Health Hero; and in 2020, she received a Princess Diana Award and was named as one of ten L'Oréal Paris Women of Worth. Chao's journey reminds me of these words that poet Amanda Gorman shared at President Joe Biden's inauguration in 2021: 'For there is always light, if only we're brave enough to see it. If only we're brave enough to be it.'

When was the last time that you wrote a thoughtful letter to someone?

When was the last time that you wrote in a journal to download and express your thoughts and feelings?

When was the last time that you put some time aside to review your day, month or year?

For many of us, the answer will either be never, or so long ago that we can't pinpoint exactly when it was. When we think about the activity of writing things down, what is more likely to come to mind is writing down reminders on Post-it notes, scribbling down a to-do list or taking notes from a meeting.

The activities of letter writing, journalling and self-reflection, however, can be life-changing, as Chao's story so beautifully illustrates.

This chapter will give you the tools to reach a higher level of consciousness and energetic awareness – journalling, questioning and gratitude. This is one of the first steps to changing your current circumstances, however fortunate or challenging they may be. You simply can't change what you're not aware of – self-development begins with better self-awareness, and becoming a curious observer of your life is how you go from just existing to truly living with energy.

One of the lessons we learn in science class at school is the first law of thermodynamics, which states that energy cannot be created or destroyed, it can only be transformed from one form to another. And while energy is a powerful force, we have the ability – through a higher level of consciousness – to direct it towards connection, change and creation. Because as we elevate our level of consciousness, we awaken to the unlimited potential of our being. The less conscious we are, however, the more energy we leak through the form of self-sabotaging behaviour that prevents us from making the progress that we would like to see.

Therapy for free

One of the first exercises that I did when committing myself to the habit of journalling was to write a letter to my younger self. It's an exercise that I get many of my clients to spend time doing. Not only is it a highly therapeutic activity, but it also helps to heal mental wounds and helps you experience a deeper sense of peace and clarity.

Get a piece of paper or a notebook out and give this a go:

1. Choose the age or period of your younger self that you would want to write to – this could be you as a child, teenager or young adult. Whoever you feel could benefit the most from reading this.
2. Take time to visualize this younger you in your mind, feeling what he or she is currently going through – the challenges, the hopes and the emotions.
3. Referring to your younger self as 'you', be as honest as you can when writing this letter. Write whatever comes to mind: words of wisdom, of comfort, of hope or of kindness.
4. Once you've finished, look at yourself in the mirror, see that younger self looking back at you, and read

out what you have written slowly and purposefully
to him or her.

5. After a few days, go through your letter with fresh
eyes, noticing what you notice.

This exercise helped me in two ways. The first is that it
helped me to reflect on just how far I had come – something
we don't do enough of in the pursuit of a better future. The
second is that what I wrote down was exactly the words that
I also needed to hear in the present. When looking back at
this letter, I saw that I highlighted this paragraph:

> It might not seem like it right now, but what you are going
> through will lead to your greatest growth. Sometimes things
> have to fall apart before they can be rebuilt in a way that sur-
> passes what came before. You can't see it now. We never can.
> But listen ever so closely and you will hear wisdom speak
> through those faint whispers in the night, those paintings of
> hope in your daydreams and those feelings shared by your
> heart. Trust this silent companion of yours – it will be an infi-
> nitely better guide than those who you seek validation from.

Writing creates this magical space around you where your
soul gets to have a meaningful conversation with itself and
allows you to get to know yourself better – your strengths,
your weaknesses, your emotions, your priorities and where
you currently are relative to where you would like to be. You
deepen your understanding about life and your role within
it. As a result, it awakens your energy to create and make
progress in the areas that spark the greatest joy from within.

Few of us take regular time to pause and explore our
thoughts without judgement. When you do, however, it will
help you understand, interpret and respond to your emotions

in a healthy way, as well as make sense of your life: to accept what has happened, understand the lessons and even redefine the meaning of an experience by seeing it from different perspectives. It provides the mind with an opportunity to breathe amid the chaos and is why many regard it as one of the most powerful activities that you can do to experience a clearer mind and a happier life.

As I so often tell my clients: you can either have a cluttered mind or cluttered books. When you transfer the clutter from your mind, which can be psychologically draining on your energy, to paper, you will experience a feeling of lightness as those heavy thoughts no longer weigh you down. What will be possible for you when your mind feels more like a peaceful oasis than one overflowing with clutter, worries and noise?

If possible, I suggest that you put your thoughts down on paper. The physical act of doing so will get you exploring your thoughts in a way that's different from typing on your smartphone or computer. You're forced to slow down and reflect on what you want to write, and to structure your thoughts and experiences in a way that helps you consider the bigger picture. Your mind is brought into the present moment as that blank space turns into a page full of words, with life breathed into them through that dance between pen and paper.

Greater self-awareness allows you to be more intentional with the choices you make each day and the impact you have on those you spend most time with. It's why understanding yourself is the beginning of wisdom. The more you understand about yourself and your current story, the better equipped you are to write a better ending.

Let us take some time now to go through some questions that will help you with this, especially if you are new to journalling. After all, we ask questions of other people nearly every day, but how often do you take the time to go inward and ask questions of yourself? Better questions lead to better answers; better answers lead to better choices; and better choices lead to better results. Grab a pen and paper, find a spot where you won't be distracted, and note down your responses to the following questions.

1. If where you would like to be in life is a 10, then on a scale of 0–10 where would you say you are at right now? What made you choose this number and not one that is higher or lower? And how will you know when you are at a number higher than where you are now?

2. What is currently draining your energy? Which of these energy leaks can you let go of in order to move forward?

3. If you had an unlimited supply of energy, what would you do with it?

4. What do you spend too much energy doing? What don't you spend enough energy doing?

5. What led you to what you are doing now with your life?

6. What is working well for you right now? What has stopped you doing more?

7. What resources do you already possess that can help you progress?

Only when you are open and honest about where you are now can you plan for the future and move forward with intention. You are surrounded by many teachers who help to shape your thinking – authors whose books you read, speakers whose words you listen to and mentors whose experience guides you – but the greatest teacher you will ever come across is life itself, and the better you get at writing and questioning, the better you get at managing your thoughts, and, in time, your journal may even take on the role of becoming your trusted spiritual guide. It will help you to evolve and grow in ways that will surprise you, by creating the space required to give birth to fresh insight and powerful breakthroughs.

Cultivate an attitude of gratitude

In July 2013, the YouTube channel SoulPancake uploaded an uplifting video sharing an experiment that they conducted on the impact of expressing gratitude. After bringing together a selection of volunteers to act as their subjects, the team got them to complete a short test to provide a measure of their current level of happiness. They were then asked to close their eyes and think of someone whom they could be deeply grateful for, someone who played an influential role in their lives or someone who did something meaningful for them that had a positive impact. Once they had identified someone, they were asked to write down as much as they could about why this person was important to them. At this point, a lot of the volunteers thought that the experiment was over, until they were really put on the spot.

The team asked each volunteer to call that person and to read out what they had written. One of them called her older sister to share the following: 'Erica is my older sister and my best friend. Sometimes it even feels like we are twins! She is my number one fan and my number one supporter. She makes me happy because despite all my mistakes and my decisions, she still loves me no matter what. Even when she has a kid and many children I will love her more than her kids! OK, maybe not. I will never forget when she flew 3,000 miles at the drop of a phone call to save me from a break-up.'

Tears, laughter and smiles appeared across the volunteers' faces as they each spoke directly to the person that they had thought of.

Before the volunteers were let go, the team gave them one more test to gauge their new level of happiness. Those who took the time to write something down but could not make the phone call for whatever reason saw their level of happiness rise 2–4%. Those who actually picked up the phone and personally expressed their gratitude saw increases of 4–19%. Either way, this experiment concluded that the act of expressing gratitude energizes us and makes us happier. And interestingly, the volunteer who experienced the greatest jump in happiness was the least happy person who walked through the door at the start.

This fun experiment was inspired by the decades of acclaimed research conducted by Dr Martin Seligman, one of the most influential psychologists in the field of happiness. He noted that when we express our gratitude to others, we strengthen our relationship with them. Too often our gratitude is expressed so casually or quickly that it feels almost meaningless. To experience the full benefits of gratitude, it's important to express it in a thoughtful and purposeful manner.

Imagine how you would feel if you were the recipient of an expression of gratitude. Visualize your manager making you feel like your work was appreciated and made a difference. A close friend sending you a short voice note to thank you for how supportive you've been. A handwritten card from a client sharing the wonderful experience they have had from working with you.

When was the last time that you expressed gratitude to someone in a meaningful way?

Gratitude is one of the fastest ways towards feeling energized when we're feeling low. It has the ability to transform a black and white day into one infused with colour. If you start expressing it more regularly, you will begin to notice just how much abundance you are surrounded by.

In her essay 'The Serviceberry – An Economy of Abundance', Robin Wall Kimmerer wrote: 'Gratitude and reciprocity are the currency of a gift economy, and they have the remarkable property of multiplying with every exchange, their energy concentrating as they pass from hand to hand, a truly renewable resource. I accept the gift from the bush and then spread that gift with a dish of berries to my neighbour, who makes a pie to share with his friend, who feels so wealthy in food and friendship that he volunteers at the food pantry. You know how it goes. To name the world as gift is to feel one's membership in the web of reciprocity.'

This web of reciprocity is what I invited a commercial lawyer client of mine, Peter, to be a part of, because in the words of William Arthur Ward, 'Feeling gratitude and not expressing it is like wrapping a present and not giving it.'

After a difficult few weeks where things had not been going his way, it was time for Peter to gain some healthy perspective to put him back on track to where he wanted to be. During our meeting, we explored all the things he could be grateful for across a number of categories that he identified as most important – his family, career, health, finances and lifestyle. As he took stock of his career, he spoke highly about Melissa – someone who took him on at a law firm fifteen years ago. She believed in him and gave him the opportunity to prove his value. It was an important moment in his life. Before the end of our meeting, I set him the challenge of handwriting a letter of gratitude to Melissa and giving it to her in person.

With the letter complete, he heads over to the company that she works for the following week to deliver it in person. However, the staff at the reception desk inform him that she retired a number of years ago.

'She must have a forwarding address?' he enquires.

'I'm afraid not,' they reply.

Peter is committed to seeing this through, so the reception staff phone around to see if anyone can forward his note on. After nearly an hour of waiting, an elderly secretary comes down to meet him, saying that it may be possible for his note to be forwarded on through a mutual contact but doesn't want to guarantee it will. With no other way to reach her, he hands the letter to this secretary and leaves. As the weeks pass and he hears nothing, he begins to wonder if she will ever get to read his words about just how grateful he is for that moment in his life.

And then one afternoon, I get a series of messages popping up on my phone from him with a sea of exclamation marks. During a training event that his company is hosting at a sports venue, he finds himself having coffee with a senior partner who he is working with on a deal. They share some jokes about the case they are working on, and before having to leave for a personal appointment, this senior partner tells him, 'Oh, by the way, Melissa got your letter and was deeply touched by it.'

Peter was gobsmacked.

It didn't matter that he couldn't hand the letter to her himself. The very fact that she received it and was able to read his expression of gratitude sent a tidal wave of happiness and energy through him.

Expressing gratitude on a regular basis not only impacts

your mental state in a positive way, it also elevates the quality of your relationships and deepens those feelings of joy and wonder.

Southwest Airlines understand this, and, in describing their culture, mention that the 'three vital elements of our culture are appreciation, recognition and celebration'. Consistently named as one of America's best employers, one of the ways they express gratitude to employees and demonstrate a high regard for them is by paying special attention to events in their personal lives – from kids' graduations to marriages and family illnesses – and recognizing these with small gestures like flowers and cards. The result? A more engaged workforce and a more profitable business.

Take a moment right now to think of someone you feel particularly grateful for.

Write down why this person came to your mind in as much detail as you can – the more specific the better.

Once you've finished doing so, put this book down and drop them a call or message to tell them what you've written about them, in the same way that the volunteers of the SoulPancake experiment did at the beginning of this chapter. If you're going through a particularly tough time right now, giving this exercise a go will more likely have a greater impact on you.

Happiness comes from seeing the extraordinary in the ordinary

After a long scenic drive along the coast at the crack of dawn, we arrived to meet our young guide, who was dressed in simple clothing and armed with a wooden stick – the sort you would imagine a martial artist making good use of in a fight.

This was the final activity that we had booked for our honeymoon week on the Indonesian island of Lombok, and it involved a challenging jungle trek to view the stunning Tiu Kelep waterfall. Once we were all introduced to each other and had soaked in the soul-soothing views of the sunrise above the distant rice fields, our guide warned us to keep any food out of sight to avoid a confrontation with the resident monkeys, before leading us deep into the lush green jungle. It didn't take long for us to discover that there was a purpose to this 'weapon' of his, as he used it to clear the path of snakes and lizards.

We navigated through ankle-deep water, climbed steep steps and hopped across uneven boulders. As the colossal sound of the waterfall pounding down on the river below grew louder in voice, our excitement mounted as we made our way over the last few boulders and through the mist-drenched air to catch our first glimpse. As the waterfall came into full view, we were awestruck by what looked to be around six waterfalls shooting out from the jungle's walls, with a more dominant one flowing down and overshadowing them from above.

After taking it in turns to swim in the crystal-clear pool beneath the waterfalls, we found a safe spot to relax and fill our stomachs with the snacks we had stuffed into our back-packs. And it was here that we got to learn a little more about our young guide.

He had just turned nineteen, and was a football fan, his favourite team being Real Madrid. He had never travelled outside Lombok and its surrounding islands. While we were amazed by the jungle that we had spent the morning hiking through, the jungle that he dreamt of moving to was a more concrete one like New York City. He even took on this job as a local guide to improve his English, after finding that watching Hollywood films could only get him so far.

We enjoyed getting to know our guide so much that by the end of his time with us we handed him the equivalent of $20 in tips and my pair of Nike shoes. He had earlier pointed to my trainers during the trek, saying that one day he would love to be able to afford a pair of shoes like mine. It was the least I could do, and I'm pretty sure it made his day, as he spun around like a dancer with a smile beaming across his face that went from ear to ear.

This humbling experience reminded me of how there's always something that we can be grateful for each day, no matter how small. As the French author Marcel Proust wrote, 'The real voyage of discovery consists not in seeking new landscapes, but in having new eyes.' In this particular moment, I felt grateful that I was in a position to be able to give a generous tip, to broaden my mind and perspective by travelling to new places, and to be able to choose my own path in life. I felt energized in the knowledge that if our guide had access to what I had, he would take full advantage of it to live the life of his dreams. It's this attitude of gratitude that turns strangers into friends, a meal into a feast and a home into a palace.

It can be so easy to complain about your life, until a meeting such as this forces you to appreciate all that you already have – to see the extraordinary in the ordinary. If you have been used to complaining about what you don't have or how others have it better than you, this can be tough at first. The reality is that we have every advantage to succeed. We take for granted all the good that is already happening in our lives, and unfortunately it's very often the case that we only truly begin to appreciate things once we've lost them.

After the sudden death of her husband from a tragic tread-mill accident while on vacation in Mexico in May 2015, Sheryl Sandberg noted: 'It is the greatest irony of my life that losing my husband helped me find deeper gratitude – gratitude for the kindness of my friends, the love of my family, the laughter of my children.' The harsh truth is that whatever rug you are standing on right now can be swept away from under your feet at any moment without notice. And while facing an unexpected crisis can derail your best-laid plans, it also acts as an important reminder not to take the simple things in life for granted.

This stark truth became a reality for so many during the global coronavirus pandemic, when the simple acts of shaking hands with a stranger, celebrating a special occasion with a large group of friends, hugging loved ones and dining out in restaurants became very quickly missed, as populations across the world retreated into their homes when lockdown measures were enforced. A question that I began asking my followers across social media as countries began lifting restrictions was, 'What is the one thing that you will never take for granted again?'

Negative visualization is an extremely powerful exercise that can teach us to value what we already have and help us realize that we are doing far better than we think we are. That no matter who we are, we possess advantages and have access to resources that others do not. It's something that the Stoic philosophers of Ancient Greece and Rome used to do regularly in order to cultivate appreciation for life in the present. By focusing on what it would feel like for important things or people to be taken away from us, we are reminded of just how fortunate we are and are energized to make full use of these blessings.

Give this exercise a go and notice the wonderful feeling that begins to radiate from within:

1. Think of something or someone that you can't live without – that if you were to lose this thing or person, your life would be severely disrupted.
2. Now close your eyes and imagine how life would be having lost the above. Visualize this scenario in as much detail as you can, noticing just how different life is.
3. Pay attention to what's missing and the impact this is having, to the emotions you are feeling and your thoughts in this moment.
4. Bring your focus back to the present and to the fact that this hasn't actually happened. Notice the gratitude you feel not just for this being an imagined scenario, but for the thing or person being in your life.

Until you are grateful for what you currently have, more will not make your life better because you will never be happy with whatever you get.

We can easily fall into the trap of destination addiction and living a conditional future – the belief that happiness can only be found in the next purchase, job, promotion or relationship. You go on this expedition to hunt down happiness, but sooner or later we learn that happiness is not found outside ourselves; it's found from within and it begins with gratitude. An ungrateful heart is a magnet for toxicity and negativity. A grateful heart, on the other hand, is a magnet for joy and positivity. If you're unhappy, be grateful, for you can't be grateful and unhappy at the same time.

Embracing a daily gratitude practice will shift your perspective and inject positive energy into every corner of your life.

It changes the lens that you view your world through, with studies consistently showing that those who practise gratitude report fewer symptoms of illness such as depression, greater feelings of optimism and happiness, stronger relationships and a desire to be kinder to others.

This clever poem, written by Chanie Gorkin when she was seventeen years old for an assignment at school in New York, illustrates this power of perspective and is titled 'Worst Day Ever?'

> Today was the absolute worst day ever
> And don't try to convince me that
> There's something good in every day
> Because, when you take a closer look,
> This world is a pretty evil place.
> Even if
> Some goodness does shine through once in a while
> Satisfaction and happiness don't last.
> And it's not true that
> It's all in the mind and heart
> Because
> True happiness can be attained
> Only if one's surroundings are good
> It's not true that good exists
> I'm sure you can agree that
> The reality
> Creates
> My attitude
> It's all beyond my control
> And you'll never in a million years hear me say
> Today was a very good day
>
> Now read it from bottom to top, the other way,
> And see what I really feel about my day.

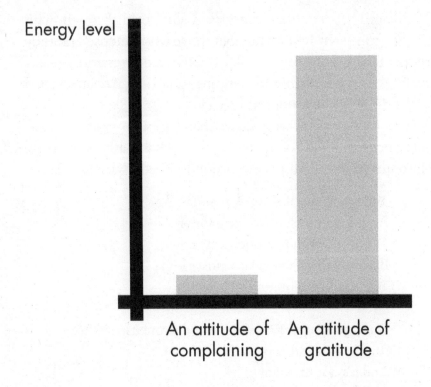

Energy level

An attitude of   An attitude of
complaining   gratitude

In a radio interview, Gorkin noted: 'I don't think there is such a thing as the worst day ever.' The objective of her poem was to show how our day is determined by how we look at things. And how we look at things can either uplift us or drain us of energy. Even when you go through challenging periods, there is still so much to be grateful for. In fact, without the bad we won't learn to appreciate all the good in our lives.

Start today to rediscover the joy that can be found in all the small things in life instead of postponing your happiness and appreciation for only those big life achievements. I promise you that when you look back one day, those small things won't be so small after all. So instead of looking for things to complain about, focus on the things you can be grateful for. For when you live from a place of gratitude, there will always be something to be grateful for.

Energy is derived from the moments of beauty, wonder and magic that we experience daily, and it's why I enjoy ending each day with a simple gratitude practice. In my journal, I note down at least one thing that I can be grateful for, in as much detail as possible, no matter how small. By the end of the week, that's a minimum of seven things that I can look back on to fill me with joy and carry over into a new week.

Discovering the extraordinary in the ordinary is what makes life worth living, as it shifts our focus away from what we lack and towards what we have. It energizes us away from limitations and towards possibilities.

To cultivate more gratitude, here's a fun challenge for you; an activity that I call creating your own GPA (Gratitude Photo Album):

1. Use your smartphone to capture moments of gratitude each day – a selfie with a friend you haven't seen for a long time, a close-up shot of your favourite meal that your partner cooked for you, or a screenshot of great feedback that you have received in your email or social media.
2. Save these to your GPA and organize by year and month.
3. At the end of each month, or when you're feeling low on energy, you can open this album and remind yourself of everything that you can be grateful for and how much good there is in your life.

How you have already won the greatest lottery there is

It took me a long time to begin talking about my mum's death openly. I was only seventeen years old when it happened, and I remember sitting next to her hospital bed holding her life-less hands, praying that she would wake from the coma that she had fallen into following an unfortunate accident. She never did.

It was a sudden, unexpected and hard lesson in the fragility of life. And I just couldn't find the words to express what I was feeling at the time. Crying was probably the closest to summarizing the pain I was experiencing, but it was some-thing I was frightened of sharing in front of people, even my closest friends. I was afraid of being judged as weak, and I knew that if my friends saw me crying, they would ask questions.

And I wasn't yet ready to tell them what had happened.

I sought refuge instead in the bathroom that my brother and I used in our family home. I would place my bath towel on the floor, lie down with my hands placed over the top of my stomach and close my eyes. As my mind started playing back memories from the times we had spent together, I would feel myself begin sinking into the floor as wave upon wave of emotion crashed over me and the tears flooded out. I would miss her French toast with strawberry jam spread across the top, the words of encouragement that she would dispense as she got me prepared for the school disco each year, and her love of pop duo Robson & Jerome's cover of 'Unchained Melody', which became the bestselling single of 1995 in the UK.

It wasn't until my second year of university that I started to feel more comfortable talking about my mum. Maybe it was a sign that I had finally accepted what had happened and wanted to do what I could to make her proud?

By acknowledging the shortness of life, you are able to channel your energy into truly living and to embrace the magic of being alive. Nothing lasts forever. We only have this one life, and the tragedy is that we wait so long to begin living it. We think we have forever, but we don't. Understanding that our stories must come to an end is what gives our lives meaning, transforms our perspective towards life and sharpens our focus on what truly matters. It gives us the opportunity to make adjustments; to use the time we have to become the person we want to be, the person we know we can be.

As Holly Butcher from Grafton, Australia, wrote in the opening paragraph of an emotionally moving post that she shared on social media one day before her death from Ewing's sarcoma – an extremely rare form of cancer that develops in the bones: 'It's a strange thing to realize and accept your mortality at twenty-six years young. It's just one of those things you ignore. The days tick by and you just expect they will keep on coming. Until the unexpected happens. I always imagined myself growing old, wrinkled and grey – most likely caused by the beautiful family (lots of kiddies) I planned on building with the love of my life. I want that so bad it hurts. That's the thing about life; it is fragile, precious and unpredictable and each day is a gift, not a given right.'

Death is not the greatest loss in life. The greatest loss is what dies inside us while we are still alive, and is why the graveyard is so often referred to as the richest place on earth, because it's filled with dreams that were never realized and talents that the world never got to benefit from.

Just as death takes what it can from life, we must focus our energy on doing exactly the same. I'm not sure who originally said this, but it instantly motivates me whenever I read it: 'Someone once told me the definition of hell: the last day you have on earth, the person you became will meet the person you could have become.'

In her book *The Top Five Regrets of the Dying*, Bronnie Ware – an Australian nurse who spent several years working in palliative care, looking after patients in the final few weeks of their lives – wrote of the phenomenal clarity of vision that people experience towards the end of their lives and how we might learn from the regrets they share if we have the humility and wisdom to do so. One day when you too are in the last few weeks of your life, you are going to really wish that you had. She highlighted some themes that surfaced again and again, with the most common regret being: 'I wish I'd had the courage to live a life true to myself, not the life others expected of me.'

Not being you, not embracing your true self, is guaranteed to lead to a heart full of regrets.

Each day is a gift and something to be deeply grateful for. Marcus Aurelius noted: 'When you arise in the morning, think of what a precious privilege it is to be alive – to breathe, to think, to enjoy, to love.' You may have woken up this morning; many people across this planet, however, didn't. When you live life with this deep feeling of gratitude, a galaxy of possibilities awaits and you discover yourself immersed in the breathtaking beauty of life like never before.

It can be easy to forget just how much of a miracle you are.

In 2020, I became a father for the first time and it was a powerful reminder to me of our existence being what scientists would label a 'miracle event'. As I held our baby, Sienna, in my arms for the very first time and gave her one of my fingers to grasp on to, I felt myself connected to a force of love that ignited an explosion of emotions within me, and was reminded of something I had read that mentioned the probability of us being born to be over 400 trillion to one. I have no idea how accurate this estimate is but I can imagine the probability being ridiculously large and perhaps even greater than their 400 trillion to one estimate.

I mean, just consider some of the following for a moment . . .

The odds that your family lineage has been completely unbroken since the beginning of human existence.

The odds of your ancestors surviving through world wars, global pandemics and then living on to reproductive age to have at least one child.

The odds of your parents meeting, staying together long enough to have children and then starting a family.

The odds that one of the trillions of sperm produced by your father successfully fused with a viable egg in your mother.

And so on.

Many in this world pin their hopes and dreams on winning the jackpot of their national or regional lottery. However, what very few truly appreciate is that we have already won the greatest lottery that there is going: the lottery of life.

You are a miracle. The question for you is this: what are you going to do with that winning ticket of yours?

3
Focus on What Matters Most

'99% of people are convinced they are incapable of achieving great things, so they aim for mediocre.'

TIM FERRISS

There comes a very important time in your life when you must reflect on whether you are really living the life that you want or not. Are you living for the weekend, spending five out of every seven days doing something that you hate, or are you content all week long? Are you floating through life merely existing or truly living as you want to? Are you settling because of fear or making changes because of a belief in a better tomorrow? Are you doing this solely for the money or because it brings fulfilment?

The time came for me to reflect on whether I was really living the life that I wanted when I was unemployed for nearly a year. It was a challenging period. The only source of income that I had, from my job in the financial services industry, had now disappeared and I was beginning to eat into my savings as each week and month passed. Despite this, it would prove to be a blessing in disguise because, as I would later learn, more often than not it is in life's hardest moments that we discover the wisdom, insight and skills to create the greatest moments of our lives. In fact, the tougher the times, the more clarity we gain about what matters most and what doesn't.

You weren't born into this world to just pay bills, scroll through social media, reply to endless emails, watch TV and then die. You were born with unique talents and gifts. And it's the greatest adventure of life to discover what these are and how you can share these with the world. There is no competition for being who you were meant to be, because there is no one else here to do exactly what you are here to do in the way that you do it. As Robert Greene wrote in his book *Mastery*, 'We are a one-time phenomenon in the universe – our exact genetic make-up has never occurred before nor will it ever be repeated.'

I shared that the period I was unemployed for was a blessing in disguise because for the first time in my life, I had the opportunity to redefine what mattered most to me. I had grown up with the belief that success was measured by my ability to land a job as a banker, doctor, lawyer or accountant and to earn a six-figure salary.

However, I soon realized that achieving this would be completely meaningless if I was living an unhappy existence as a result. Since work fills up a large part of our lives, I didn't want to be spending my time working for things which simply didn't matter. I didn't want to make progress in something that I secretly wished was something else. Life is far too short and precious not to pursue something that brings out the absolute best in you, and you can't live your best life or produce your greatest work if you don't like what you do.

In many cases, the reason we are exhausted is because we are caught up in trying to run someone else's race and live up to their definition of success.

We must take responsibility for where we are and where we want to be. No more blaming, no more excuses. Rather than continue to wonder when your life might begin, you can choose to start living right now and to let go of a way of life that you may have settled for. If I didn't make the time to start creating a life that I wanted, I knew that I would be forced to spend a lot more time dealing with an undesirable one. This wasn't going to be me. I wanted to live an energetic life that was aligned with my values. As a result, I began to reflect on the following questions, which I've since used with many of my coaching clients. I suggest that you write down everything that comes to mind as you read through each of them, as doing so will help you get the most from what comes next in this chapter.

1. What does success mean to you?
2. What does fulfilment look like to you?
3. What sort of impact do you want your life to have?
4. What would you do if money were no object?

Too many of us are flying at a level far below our true potential and it's why we must get clear on what we want in life and stop living on autopilot, hoping that someone other than ourselves will swoop down and carry us towards the promised land.

We must therefore make time to go inward to reflect on our own definitions and then have the courage to build our lives around those answers. Your vision will become clear only when you look into your heart. Who looks outside, dreams; who looks inside, awakens,' said the psychiatrist Carl Jung. It's because no one knows you better than you know yourself.

To live in this way – with purpose – is to unlock one of the greatest sources of energy that there is, and to arrive here requires you to embark on the longest journey you will ever make: that from your head to your heart. Whatever you want to call it – your heart, gut, intuition or true self – make sure you pay attention to what it has to say, even if it's a soft whisper. It may not always be right, but it will always guide you to where you need to be. And when we fail to listen to it, we often end up being a fraction of the person that we were meant to be. Every hero needs a guide; let your heart be yours.

When you're clear on what success means to you and you care about what you're working towards, you will show up with vastly more energy in the form of creativity, focus and persistence. Because when a compelling vision pulls you forward, you no longer have to rely on pushing yourself to get things done. And the more magnetic that vision is, the easier it is to avoid unnecessary distractions and transcend any fear you may have.

Remember when you first fell in love? You gave little thought to much else as you found the energy to spend as much time as possible with them, even if it meant cancelling plans that you already made with others. When you love something, you will give everything you have for it and living with purpose is no different. You find yourself stepping away from the sidelines and into the life that you know you are meant to live.

Before we move forward, I want you to take a moment to reflect on these questions: What story are you currently living and what story do you want to be living?

The magnetic energy of a compelling vision

In 1969, he was unknown to the world and struggling financially. He was only able to get small supporting roles on TV
at a time when his second child, Shannon, was born and when
he had to fight racism within his industry. And circumstances
would suddenly get more challenging, as his role in a new
show, *The Green Hornet*, lasted just one season.

He felt that he was destined for more – that he had so much
more to give to the world and that there was a story inside
him waiting to be told.

Sitting down, he took out a fresh sheet of paper, stamped
the word SECRET at the top and bottom, and did something that so few of us will ever do. Titled 'My Definite
Chief Aim', he wrote down the following words as a way of
programming a focus deep into the inner landscape of his
subconscious:

> I, Bruce Lee, will be the first highest paid Oriental super star
> in the United States. In return I will give the most exciting
> performances and render the best of quality in the capacity
> of an actor. Starting 1970 I will achieve world fame and from
> then onwards till the end of 1980 I will have in my possession
> $10,000,000. I will live the way I please and achieve inner
> harmony and happiness.

Each day, he would read these words, visualize this aim
unfolding in the invisible world of his mind and feel the energetic intensity of this future as if it was being experienced
today. He was writing and speaking this imagined world into
existence.

A year later, on his return to Hong Kong from San

Francisco, he discovered that the show he had appeared on for just one season in the US had become a runaway success. Unofficially referred to as *The Kato Show*, he was surprised to be recognized as the star of the show. Studio bosses in Hong Kong were fighting for his name, and this led to a series of films such as *Fist of Fury* and *Way of the Dragon*. In fact, these two films alone went on to gross an estimated $100 million and $130 million worldwide, respectively. In the process, he was catapulted to stardom. And this newfound status led to Warner Brothers offering him the opportunity in 1972 to star in his own Hollywood blockbuster, *Enter the Dragon*.

Within just four years of writing that letter to himself and before his life was tragically cut short at just thirty-two years old, he had achieved everything that he wrote down. The energetic intensity of his thoughts had flowed into the physical form of his daily actions.

Lee isn't the only human to have benefited from getting clear about what he wanted and what he was willing to give in return for it. There have been countless others who have made the audacious decision to reflect on what they truly want and write down in specific detail the same exact information. Stories such as this remind me of these words of Paulo Coelho in *The Alchemist*: 'When you want something, all the universe conspires in helping you to achieve it.'

How big you play in life is entirely up to you.

The bigger you play, however, the more you will come to realize that the real benefit of having a compelling vision is less about what you get and more about who you become in the process of translating those energetic thoughts into reality.

Author and educationalist Sir Ken Robinson pointed out that, 'For most of us the problem isn't that we aim too high

and fail. It is just the opposite: we aim too low and succeed.'
Most of us aim for something that is easy to achieve. To live
an extraordinary life, however, you mustn't be afraid to dream
bigger, use your imagination and connect with your inner
child, because limitations only exist in the minds of those who
are not brave enough to dream the impossible.

Many are too short-term in their thinking – their field of
vision going only so far as the end of this month's paycheque
or their next holiday. Dreaming big requires you to think long-
term, however, to work backwards from an exciting vision
and not your next paycheque or holiday.

The following is an exercise that I get my coaching clients
to do during our first session together, and is something that
will also help you to get clear on what matters most to you.
The key here is to think without limitation. Don't rush through
it if you want to get the most from this – go into as much
detail as you can, because if what you write is too vague, you
will find it difficult to visualize.

1. Imagine that you and I were to meet five years from
   today and you were to tell me, 'Simon, the last five
   years have been the most incredible and magical of
   my life in every way. It hasn't been easy for sure, but
   I can honestly say that I am the happiest and
   healthiest I have ever been – both from a personal
   and professional perspective.'

2. What would you be telling me has happened that
   has contributed to these five years being the most
   incredible? Write this down now in as much detail as
   you can. The more specific, the better.

   • What accomplishments are you most proud of?
   • What does your personal life now look like?

- Where are you living and who are you spending your time with?
- How much money are you now earning and how is this being used?
- In what ways have you shown up as your true self?
- How has your physical and mental health improved?
- What has been the greatest challenge you have overcome?
- What are you now doing that you previously didn't think possible?
- What have been the most important changes you have made in your life?
- What important lessons have the last five years taught you?

3. Review what you have written to see if there's anything else you want to add before reflecting on what all of this tells you, especially with regard to what matters most.

Until you have this clarity on what matters most, it's difficult to get excited about the journey that lies ahead because prioritizing becomes impossible. Since most won't do this self-reflection work, many will waste their time and energy tiptoeing through life feeling busy but going nowhere because they lack direction. We can only be intentional with how we live each day when we have something compelling that pulls us forward, because it is this passion for the extraordinary that unleashes our energetic self.

When you possess a clear and compelling vision of what you desire, however, you begin to notice opportunities that most are not even aware of. This is because your subconscious has been called upon by your conscious to focus its energy and attention on something specific. And the more specific it is, the more believable it will be to you. Without this, you will lack intrinsic motivation. Possessing a compelling vision sets the stage for everything that you want to manifest in your life. You have to see yourself live that life before you can have that life, such that you are constantly challenging your reality to catch up with what you have constructed in the domain of your mind.

Having a vision that demonstrates magnetic qualities not only unlocks a powerful source of personal energy and gives us something to focus our attention on, it can also attract others to the cause, especially when that vision is greater than our individual selves.

This is what helped Lockheed's chief engineer, Clarence 'Kelly' Johnson, and his small team of engineers and mechanics to deliver the impossible in 1943. During the Second World War, the Nazi regime introduced the world's first operational jet-powered fighter, which was much faster and better armed than any plane in the Allied arsenal. The prospect of these planes dominating the skies over Europe filled the US Department of Defense with absolute terror. They needed a counterpunch and fast. This was when they turned to Kelly, and despite his bosses at Lockheed regarding the project as nothing more than fantasy, given the proposed 180-day turnaround, Kelly accepted the mission.

No company had ever designed and built any kind of prototype in anywhere near that kind of time, let alone a prototype for a jet fighter. The time pressures would be intense. But this was different. This was a top-secret assignment with a bold vision: to save the world from the Nazi threat. It would be the greatest challenge in American aviation, with a mission that would bring everyone together, united behind and energized by a common purpose. They were engaged and driven by the fact that their work would contribute to the success of such an important goal. While his superiors remained sceptical, Kelly got to work. And 143 days later, on 15 November 1943, an incredible thirty-seven days ahead of schedule, he delivered America's first military jet.

My message to you here is to be bold in your thinking when it comes to scribing down your vision. To see what can be, not just what is. By doing so, you also become an energizer for others in the same way that Kelly was for his team. During a visit to India in 2014, Microsoft CEO Satya Nadella told a hall full of students: 'The energy you create around you is going to be the most important attribute you bring to others. I do believe in the long run EQ does trump IQ. For without the ability to be a source of energy for others, very little can be accomplished.' Nadella explained that having genuine passion and enthusiasm for what you do is important when pursuing leadership qualities, for leaders create energy.

You don't need a fancy title or to be in a position of power in order to begin demonstrating leadership qualities. You can decide to act like a leader today, in every area of your life. And when you pursue a vision that means something to you with passion, your energy and enthusiasm will be infectious. You will exhibit an excitement for life that will be difficult to ignore, and from this state of feeling supercharged, just imagine all that you will be able to accomplish.

Unlock supercharged abilities through the power of visualization

The practice of visualization is nothing new in the world of sport, and it's something that elite athletes have been practising as part of their mental training for many years. Prior to Roger Bannister breaking the four-minute mile in 1954, for example, experts considered the human body incapable of doing so. It was regarded as an impossibility. As part of his training, however, he was relentless in visualizing his ability to run a mile and cross that finish line in under four minutes. The frequency with which he did so created a sense of certainty within him that it would happen and, as a result, energized his mind and body.

And ahead of the FIFA Women's World Cup Final in 2015, hosted in Canada, Carli Lloyd of the US women's soccer team said that she mentally visualized herself scoring four goals. She went on to score three goals within the first sixteen minutes of the final against Japan – the first woman in World Cup history to do so – and noted in her post-game interviews how she had taken visualization to another level to help her feel energized both mentally and physically. According to Lloyd, 'If your mental state isn't good enough, you can't bring yourself to bigger and better things.'

When you bring together a clearly defined vision with the act of visualization, you begin to live every moment in a state of absolute certainty that you will achieve it.

Creating a mental picture of your future and not focusing on your past will help you to turn possibility into reality. Visualizing the energetic state that you want to be in or something that you want to achieve will fill you with the energy you need to begin sculpting it into reality; to turn the goals you have written down and repeated to yourself into the life that you desire. Visualization helps you to focus on what is important and therefore stops you wasting your energy on the things that aren't as important to you. In short, visualization primes your mind for success and adds emotional depth to your plans.

Our body is, in effect, being immersed in the emotions of what the future will feel like ahead of the actual experience taking place. And it lights us up with energy, which in turn unleashes a driving force or fire that can unlock our abilities. It's what the Indian philosopher Patanjali was pointing to when he said: 'When you are inspired by some great purpose, some extraordinary project, all your thoughts break their bonds. Your mind transcends limitations, your consciousness expands in every direction and you find yourself in a new, great and wonderful world. Dormant forces, faculties and talents become alive and you discover yourself to be a greater person by far than you ever dreamed yourself to be.'

While the practice of visualization in the world of sport is obvious and well-studied, it's a powerful tool that we can also embrace in the achievement of our personal and career-related goals. This is an important step that you must practise daily if you want to move faster along the journey of making the vision you wrote down earlier in this chapter a reality, because you must be able to see it in your mind first before you can achieve it. This process of emotionalizing your vision will provide you with the energy and insights to transform the way you live and work.

If you didn't take the time earlier to flesh out your five-year vision and what matters most in detail, then go back now and do that because you will need it for this visualization exercise.

Since a version of this is something that I usually guide my clients through via a recording that I share with them, you may want to have someone read this out to you, pausing for at least fifteen seconds after each step.

1. Close your eyes, take a few deep breaths to relax your mind and bring to mind the vision of your ideal future that you wrote down as if you have already achieved it.
2. Make these images as sharp and as vivid as you can, noticing how confident, fulfilled and happy you are.
3. Look at your surroundings and notice who else is there with you. Listen to what they are saying to you and what you are saying to yourself.
4. Bring your attention now to what you are doing and how you are doing it. More importantly, notice how you are feeling in this moment.
5. Let this incredible feeling cover you like a blanket, bathing your entire body in these wonderful sensations.
6. From this energetic state of being, reflect on what words of wisdom this confident, fulfilled and happy you would say to the you of today. Listen closely to what is shared.
7. When you're ready, slowly begin to open your eyes. As you do, notice how you are feeling more energized and ready to act on what matters most.

Once you're familiar with these steps, you can use them at any moment to activate your superconscious mind. Do this daily and you will begin to programme your magnetic vision deeper and deeper into your subconscious; the result of which will be your ability to see opportunities that you were previously blind to. This happens because of the truth that you become what you constantly think about and get what you focus your energy on.

Fail to plan, plan to fail

A big dream. An audacious goal. An inspiring legacy.

These are all important, but without some plan in place, you aren't setting yourself up for success. If you want to avoid living life by default, you must be strategic with how you use your time, because intentional choices always lead to better outcomes. To make quantum leaps forward, you must therefore sit down, plan those stepping stones and then get to work on that plan. As my friend Musa Tariq (CMO at GoFundMe) shared in a social media post: 'I bet most of you have never sat down for at least an hour with a blank piece of paper and mapped out your career, what's important to you and what your life strategy is, yet you probably do it for the company you work for all the time. Telling, isn't it. Focus on you this weekend.'

Your ability to reflect, make plans and then actually follow through on them will become one of the greatest skills that you will come to master.

Mastering this skill not only turns you into a productivity machine but it gives you something to look forward to each day. It helps you to wake up each morning to the smell of possibilities.

In his book *What They Don't Teach You at Harvard Business School*, Mark McCormack shared a study conducted between 1979 and 1989 on Harvard's MBA graduates. The study asked them, in 1979, just one question: 'Have you set clear, written goals for your future and made plans to accomplish them?'

From those asked, 84% said that they didn't have specific goals in mind aside from their summer plans, 13% said they had goals in mind but they were not in writing, and just 3% said that they had clear, written goals with a plan on how to accomplish them.

The researchers interviewed the same students from this graduating class again ten years later, in 1989, to measure their progress. The results were staggering. The 13% who had goals in mind but with no written plans or strategy on how to achieve them were earning, on average, twice as much as the 84% who had no clear goals. And the 3% who had set clear, written goals with a plan to accomplish them? They were earning, on average, ten times as much as the other 97% of their class combined.

When I get my clients to show me their calendars, I see that they have blocked out time for others: meetings with colleagues, with partners, with friends or with clients. However, when I ask them, 'What time have you blocked out for you – a meeting with yourself to plan out your career and life strategy?' I often get a puzzled look followed by the response that they don't have the time.

And here's what I tell them: 'You don't have time because it's not scheduled in your calendar and unless you schedule it, you'll never do it. If it's a priority for you, then you will schedule it with the same energy that you schedule time to watch that show on Netflix, to plan that next holiday with your family and to organize that night out with friends. In fact, when you say you don't have time, what you are really telling me is that it's not your priority right now.'

If you purchased this book with the desire to change your current circumstances, then bring up your calendar now and block out at least an hour in the next week to have a one-on-one meeting with yourself to map out a strategy for your career and life.

'Most people allow their lives to simply happen to them,' wrote John C. Maxwell in his book *The 15 Invaluable Laws of Growth*. 'They float along. They wait. They react. And by the time a large portion of their life is behind them, they realize they should have been more proactive and strategic.' Don't be like most people. You may not be able to travel back in time and change what has already happened, but you can certainly begin today to change the trajectory of your tomorrow.

When I was planning my exit from employment so that I could concentrate my energy on building my business, one of the techniques that I employed was that of questionstorming. Unlike brainstorming, where the objective is to generate ideas and solutions, questionstorming is focused on generating a series of questions for us to act upon.

Here are some of the questions that I came up with at the time during those one-on-one meetings with myself:

- What are the most important skills I must learn in order to start a successful business, and how will I develop these?
- What pricing structure would I be comfortable using as I build my experience?
- What are the challenges ahead that I foresee and how do I plan to overcome them?
- What strengths can I draw upon and how will I apply them?
- How can I start at once to give people an experience of what I do?
- How can I prioritize more time in my week to dedicate to what I want to do longer-term?

- How can I stand out from the competition and get people interested in what I offer?
- How can I expand my network to be surrounded by those who share similar values?
- How will I know that I am making good progress ninety days from today?
- Who can I reach out to that I can learn or seek guidance from?

I then took time to reflect on each of these questions in my journal, with action steps emerging as a result and scheduled into my calendar. This process of proper planning saves you energy because there are now fewer decisions for you to make, and as a result, you make more productive use of your time each day. Give this exercise a go for yourself, using your vision as a reference point, and see what questions you can come up with. Answering questions like these ignites your creative energy and provides you with clarity on where to direct your attention. It's an incredibly important step on your path towards living an energized and fulfilled life. How you use your hours each day determines whether your vision will be realized or not. You need an energizing vision. But you must not get so distracted by it that you forget that the results you want are determined by how your energy is being spent today.

As we come to the end of the first part of this book, it's important for us to reflect on what we have covered so far. We began by exploring why we must invest in our health if we want to have a solid foundation of energy in place to transform our future. We then touched on the powerful impact that journalling and gratitude can have on our mental energy by elevating our level of consciousness. And we ended by spending time getting clear on what matters most and how to tap into the wonders of visualization so that we can focus our energy on the right things.

By now, you will have ideas on how to improve your health, a better understanding about yourself and where you currently are, deeper feelings of joy from embracing an attitude of gratitude and clarity on what your ideal future looks like. The next part of the book will show you how to rewire your energetic state so that you're able to create an unstoppable mindset.

AWAKEN

Stop treating your health as a side hustle. Reflect on how you want to feel today. Get more sleep. Wake up full of energy. Embrace an active lifestyle. Exercise to energize. Eat smarter. Cut down on the alcohol; become a waterholic. Cultivate an attitude of gratitude. Express your appreciation to others in thoughtful ways. Remind yourself of how much of a miracle you are. Take time to reflect, write and deepen your level of self-awareness. Be more proactive and strategic with your life. Have courage to build your life around what matters most. Thing big, act bold and take responsibility for where you are and where you want to be.

PART 2

Rewire Your Energetic State

4
Break Free of Your Energetic Blocks

'The energy of the mind is the essence of life.'

ARISTOTLE

As I logged on to my university's website, the realization that my nightmares were now very much a reality began to sink in. Since I put my pen down on that final exam paper, this moment of discovering what my results were had weighed heavily on my mind and, as a result, kept me awake for months. I had a feeling that I did badly – the question was, how badly?

From childhood to adulthood, I had observed that failure was punished and looked down upon, while success was rewarded and looked up to. It led to a need for me to feel successful in the eyes of my parents and peers. As a result, I had anchored my self-worth to exam results, getting into a good university and landing a job that paid a high salary.

I sat four exams that year – I just about scraped a pass in

one of them and failed the other three. This meant that I had to now repeat my second year and that a three-year under-graduate degree would now become a four-year one. My primary concern, however, was about how I was going to share this news with my dad and the rest of the family. They were waiting downstairs, ready to celebrate and congratulate me on what they expected were going to be stellar results. The champagne was even in the ice bucket.

I've let them down.

I'm a failure.

I've destroyed my future.

I've wasted a year of my life.

These were the thoughts that were running through my head.

My dad had made the 7,106-mile trip from Sibu, Malaysia, to London, England, in pursuit of a better university education. Given how poor the family was, it wasn't an easy choice. Eventually, however, his parents reluctantly agreed, and he got himself a one-way ticket to London with £100 in his pocket.

To make ends meet, he had to self-fund as much as he could, and despite only speaking broken English on arrival, he was taken in by a friend's aunt and uncle who looked after him. When not busy studying, he worked multiple part-time jobs, with the energy to do so driven by his determination to make a success of his education.

Knowing this made me feel ashamed and embarrassed about the news I was about to break to them.

As I walked down the stairs of my uncle's house, my facial expression and body language communicated what had hap-pened before I uttered a single word. They were shocked and disappointed that I had failed as spectacularly as I had. We can suffer more in our imagination than in reality, and while the initial reaction was expected, they were later encouraging with their words and advice.

Despite this, the event shattered my confidence. It killed my energetic state and negatively influenced the beliefs that I had about myself. It made me question my value and whether I had much of a future ahead of me – something that was made worse when I was comparing my situation to others who had seamlessly sailed into the next year of university and had already landed multiple job offers. Knowing what I know now, I understand just how dangerous being afflicted by comparisonitis can be. It's the enemy of happiness, the thief of joy and an energy killer, whose sole purpose is to make you feel less satisfied with your own life.

We often think of energy in terms of just the physical, but our mental energy also plays an important role when it comes to our energetic state. How you experience the world is a mirror of your mental energy, since your reality is created from the inside out, not the outside in.

To achieve more in life, therefore, you must learn how to master your energetic state, so that your mind is working for you and not against you. Doing so will help you understand that happiness and fulfilment are less about your degree, job or title and more about living with purpose, while being kinder to yourself and evolving into the person that you were meant to be. When we tie our self-worth to something or someone outside of ourselves, we lose sight of the multiple blessings we already have in our lives and stack energetic blocks in front of us that stop us from enjoying periods of flow. Given that we have limited mental energy each day, we must also be mindful not to waste it on things that we have absolutely no control over.

When we think about our state of being, energetic blocks are mental obstructions to being in flow – a closed mind, a fixed belief system and a lack of faith in our abilities. They keep you from living a meaningful life and achieving your dreams. Think of energetic blocks like sunglasses. The longer you keep them on, the less you notice how everything appears darker than it actually is. When you're operating from this lower frequency, it's difficult to think positive, and when the universe does deliver you a sign or wake-up call, your first response is to punch that snooze button. You don't give yourself the opportunity to even try. When you operate at a higher frequency and an energetic state of positivity, however, you are able to thrive regardless of external circumstances – turning setbacks into strength and obstacles into opportunities – and are open to new experiences that help you grow.

Look at how children behave, and you will notice how flow is very much our natural state of being. Their minds are focused on the now, like a sponge that has a thirst for learning, and equipped with an imagination that is energized by possibilities over limitations. Their minds are free of energetic blocks. When told that this is just the way things are, their minds ask, 'Why?' And when told that they can't do something, their minds ask, 'Why not?'

Take four-year-old Austin Perine (also known as President Austin), whose inspiring idea came to him after watching a baby panda on TV. During this animal show, the mother panda was leaving her cubs and Perine was told that the panda would be homeless. He didn't know what the word 'homeless' meant, and his dad said that it was somebody who didn't have a home or a parent around. And to show him the meaning of the word, he was taken to see the local city shelter. By the end of that day, Perine ended up feeding all the homeless people there.

Since then, he has attracted the support of his country – from brands to government organizations – to help him in his mission not to let the homeless go hungry and to encourage everyone to show love. He is often seen doing so while wearing his superhero cape, exchanging hugs and fist bumps. What energizes him longer-term is a vision of building a facility that addresses the many causes of homelessness. If you think of your energy like a magnet, then when you are in flow you are attracting more energy into your life. When your mind is contaminated with energetic blocks, however, you are repelling energy from your life in the form of opportunities and relationships.

I often tell clients that there are always two sells that occur – the second is selling yourself to others and the first is selling you to you. Without addressing the first, the second will always remain a challenge. For me to sell myself to myself, I had to release the unhelpful thoughts that were blocking my flow and to stop watering the destructive thinking patterns stunting my growth. This part of the book will show you how I went about doing so and how rewiring my energetic state in this manner allowed me to be kinder to myself and to embrace beliefs that have helped me to flourish, and how you can too.

You are both the sculpture and the sculptor

We act consistently with who we believe we are. If you believe that you are a victim, you will attract opportunities into your life that will allow you to play out that role. If you believe that you can't do much, your mind will seek out reasons to support that belief of yours. When you believe in yourself, in your capabilities, and that a better future is possible, however, you unlock the doors to an ocean of possibilities, unleash levels of energy you never knew existed and awaken the creative spirit that we are all born with.

The mind is a truly powerful force. It can make you feel like a victim or empower you, it can plunge you down into the depths of misery or lift you up into the realm of superhuman achievement. Use this power wisely.

You get back what you put out in the world, and what you put out is driven by the beliefs that you hold. It is what creates the customized reality that we each live in.

You can't expect others to see your value if you don't first see it for yourself, so never underestimate the impact of being the first to believe in yourself and your potential. Without the right mindset, you simply won't see the abundance of opportunities and possibilities that surround us all and that only reveal themselves to you when your level of energy and vibration matches that of what you desire. For this to occur you must believe your vision is possible and be able to experience what it would feel like at an emotional level when it becomes your reality. Since we attract what we are, we are always a vibrational match to our current reality.

When the apprentice in the popular Chinese parable asks his master, 'When is the best time to plant a tree?' and is told 'Twenty years ago', but that if he missed that chance, his second best is right now, it is a lesson that we can take note of for our own lives. Something may have stopped you from planting your tree all those years ago, but what if you could plant that tree today and take meaningful steps forward to positively change the future course of your life?

We all have magic within us, but the world will never get to see any of it if you continue to give in to your energetic blocks and play small because you are too afraid of changing or letting go of what no longer serves you. 'Our deepest fear is not that we are inadequate,' wrote Marianne Williamson in her book *A Return to Love*. 'Our deepest fear is that we are powerful beyond measure. It is our light, not our darkness that most frightens us.' For you to open up to your power and light, you must disrupt the mindless thought patterns that are blocking you from making progress towards what matters most.

What separates those who go on to achieve and those who feel imprisoned by doubt is the belief that they can figure things out. It is this level of self-belief that fuels our energy. Without this belief in yourself, you are almost guaranteed to fail in any endeavour. Begin today to change the way you see yourself, to regularly remind yourself that you are far stronger than you think you are, and witness how your entire life begins to transform. Don't wait another twenty years, wishing that you could've planted your tree today.

When you think a thought, your mind transmits this information, which carries within it either a positive or negative energy charge, down to the rest of your body. And depending on its contents, your body will respond accordingly. It's how monks can sit peacefully and lightly dressed in their robes despite the low temperatures of their surroundings that would make most shiver. It's how we begin to feel warm and sweaty when we think we have lost our passport on our way to the airport or when we do something new for the very first time that pulls us out of our comfort zone. The outside temperature hasn't changed, but that of our bodies as a result of our thinking has.

Internal belief always precedes external achievement – it's in this transference of energy that the physical equivalent of thought is generated and sculpted, the formless creating form.

In fact, your behaviour in the present is largely determined by the view that you have for your future. Only when your future is clear, exciting and something that you believe is possible can your actions and behaviour in the present reflect that. If you don't believe that a better future is possible, you are putting up energetic blocks that can only result in low-energy emotions. Circumstances don't determine your future, your beliefs about what those circumstances mean do.

It's important for us to reflect on the beliefs in every area of our lives that are driving our current reality, so that we may assess whether they are contributing to or blocking our progress, because this invisible world of beliefs affects our world in more ways than we can imagine through the actions that we take or don't take. And the greater your self-belief, the more intense your actions will be and the more in flow you will feel. They are like a hidden script running in the background of our lives and directing the quality of our relationships with everything from money to others and to ourselves. We are creatures of habit, so to break free of the energetic blocks currently holding us back, we must change our thought patterns.

Nearly all the beliefs that you hold have been made up or inherited from someone else, and when you realize that you can choose a new belief at any moment, you can begin the process of creating new ones – of letting go of those that no longer serve you so that you can make space for the planting of more empowering seeds of thought. The sort that allows us to slowly crack that ceiling of self-doubt and tear open the portal to the hero potential within us all.

Here's a powerful exercise that helped me to move forward and that I use with clients to raise their awareness around the nature of thought so that they can go from facing energetic blocks to being in energetic flow – something that can only occur when a mind is open and not closed.

1. Write down a belief that is currently blocking you from making the progress you would like towards the vision you identified earlier in the book. Maybe you think you're too old (or too young), you can't earn money doing what you really love, you need to work all the hours of the day in order to make a success of your career or you're not good with money.
2. Write down what this belief has cost you in the past and what you have lost because of it.
3. Write down what this belief is costing you in the present and what you are losing because of it.
4. Write down what this belief will cost you five years from today and what you will lose because of it.
5. Write down what would happen if the opposite of this belief were true and what would happen as a result.
6. Write down three facts or pieces of evidence that could support this more empowering belief.
7. Visualize what your life looks like operating from this new belief, noticing how it impacts the lives of people around you.

What we accomplish in life is only limited by the stories we tell ourselves, since they guide our actions and, in turn, our identity. And our identity is simply the sum of the stories that we are telling ourselves at any given moment about our past, our present and our future. As you break free of the blocks that have held you back, you allow your energetic force to radiate out into the world from within.

Choose your words carefully

Over the course of a day, we have around 60,000 thoughts, many of which come and go so quickly that we're not even aware of them. Most people aren't even aware of the chatter going on inside their heads. While some thoughts are positive and empowering, how many are negative, catastrophizing in nature or block you from fulfilling your potential?

According to an article published by the National Science Foundation, 80% of these thoughts tend to be negative and 95% precisely the same repetitive thoughts that were experienced the day before. All of this results in a serious leakage and waste of vital energy. These are just some of the most common thoughts that I often hear, which have held people back from fulfilling their potential:

- 'It's just too much of a challenge to overcome given my circumstances.'
- 'I should just give up. There's too much competition.'
- 'I don't deserve to be there. What experience do I have?'
- 'There's no point starting. It's just too much work and it's not guaranteed to work out.'

What do you feel speaking these words to yourself would do to your energy?

We have all these opportunities throughout the day to build ourselves up, and the first step to taking them with both hands is by understanding how our internal dialogue affects our lives because we ultimately get what we feel we deserve. Just imagine what you can do and achieve when you believe you are actually worth it; when you silence that inner critic and instead listen to the words of the guide within. You might not be able to control what people think of you, but you can always control the way you think about yourself.

Be careful about the words that you choose to follow on from 'I am', for they will always come looking for you. Our mind always believes whatever we tell it. If your thoughts are dominated by words that make you feel you're not enough, then you'll always act from this place of being, because negative energy attracts negative energy. It's this sort of self-talk that dulls your energetic state. On the other hand, if your mind is flooded by uplifting thoughts and words, it leads to living each day with purpose and abundance, since positive energy attracts positive energy. Your life moves in the direction of your most dominant thoughts, and because they have the power to determine your reality, you must fuel your mind with thoughts of a higher frequency if you are to enjoy an energy-rich life.

How you think determines how you act through the energetic state that you are supporting; it's the domino effect in action, with thought as its catalyst. It breathes life into your energetic state or sucks the life out of it. And it all begins by having healthier conversations with yourself.

The most powerful dialogue is the one that happens within yourself every day, because what consumes your thinking influences who you become. The quality of your energetic state is directly linked to the conversations you have with yourself. If you want to rewire your energetic state so that it serves you rather than limits you, then it's important that you speak to yourself in the same way you would to someone you deeply care about, for the person that you will speak to the most in your lifetime is you.

As Brianna Wiest writes in her book *Ceremony*, 'You fall in love with yourself when you start to take care of yourself. You fall in love with yourself when you stop thinking of self-love as an infatuation, but a homecoming. You fall in love with yourself when the child inside looks at the adult you are now and sees the ease of their own approval.' It is self-compassion, not self-criticism, that gives you the energy to be comfortable with the uncomfortable.

We all have doubts about ourselves, and while it's impossible to eliminate negative thoughts in their entirety, a greater awareness around the contents of your thinking and their impact on your behaviour can help you reframe these into more positive thoughts. Living life at a higher frequency of energy doesn't mean that there's an absence of fear; it's the belief that you will be fine despite your fears. No relationship is more important than the one you have with yourself. We deal with our mind from the second we wake to the second we sleep, so being aware of how you speak to yourself is the first step in shifting your mind from being your worst enemy to your best friend.

Words matter – they have the power to energize, to soothe, to heal and to hurt. A single sentence can be life-changing in its ability to make or break potential. Tell yourself that 'I don't have a single artistic bone in my body', and it will be a very long time before you find the courage to start creating. Tell yourself that 'I love painting and so am going to just start creating and see where it takes me', and you start sharing your gift immediately with a sense of childlike wonder and without judgement. And it is this focus on creation that ultimately leads to mastery within any domain of work.

If you want to rewrite the narrative of where your story goes from here, you must change how you speak to yourself. 'When we start to pay attention, we notice how quickly the critic jumps in, even when something good happens,' writes

Sharon Salzberg in *How to Recognize Your Inner Critic*. 'If people befriend us, our critic may whisper that if they only knew how insecure and defective we are, they wouldn't stick around for long. Or say you've just run a marathon. Are you celebrating the fact that you trained, ran and finished? Or are you upbraiding yourself for being the last person to cross the finish line?'

You don't need a degree in physics to understand that what you focus your energy on expands – when you give your energy to certain thoughts, they gain life and will either carry you closer to where you want to be or ground you in mediocrity.

It's something that I often have to remind my clients of so that they can overcome their energetic blocks. When Oliver first enquired about working together to help him switch careers into the social impact space from nearly two decades as an employee working for a global marketing agency, I heard a lot of self-doubt during our first meeting:

ME: What has stopped you making the switch?

OLIVER: I have done well in this career, Simon. It has taken many years and sacrifices to have got to where I am. I'm just not sure if I'll be throwing all this away for something that I have no clue is going to work or not.

ME: No clue that it's going to work or not?

OLIVER: Exactly. It's a huge risk going from the stability of a full-time job that I have been successful in to starting my own business. Don't get me wrong, the idea of it working out is exciting. But I'm also a realist.

ME: I'm curious, Oliver. You relocated from South Africa to the UK to take on a role at this company that you're still with today. How much of a risk was this for you at the time?

OLIVER: A big risk. I was leaving family and friends behind for something that I couldn't have predicted to turn out as well as it has. It was a different decision to the one I'm facing now though, because it felt like the next step in my career journey. The salary was attractive and, in many ways, it was like I was embarking on an exciting adventure.

ME: What if this switch from working for someone to working for yourself is the next step in your life journey?

OLIVER: That's an interesting thought.

ME: Let's assume for a moment that it is the next step in your life journey, what must now happen?

OLIVER: I've already started to build some relationships within the social impact space outside of work hours. I've just got to decide whether to focus all my energy on it or not. If I don't, I'm not going to make much progress. If I do, I could be in a situation where I no longer have job security and where the business isn't paying me enough to survive.

ME: What if it did work out better than you could ever imagine?

OLIVER: A lot would then be possible! I mean, I would have more time to spend with family and friends, feel happier and be energized to take on all those other ideas that I've been thinking about. There would be a sense of freedom and lightness that I haven't had for a long while.

ME: A sense of adventure perhaps?

OLIVER: Yes! Exactly that.

ME: You know, Oliver, our minds can often trick us into thinking that we want comfort when what we really want is adventure. You relocated to a new country with no guarantee that the move would work out; it appears now that it worked out very well. Your curiosity around the social impact space gave you the energy to begin exploring this area, despite working in a demanding job. And when you shared with me earlier that you've found it difficult to sleep recently, I wonder if it's because of a feeling from within telling you that you have outgrown where you currently are?

OLIVER: I think you're right. I feel like what's important to me has changed and, as a result, my definition of success has evolved. It led me to you, and I know this is what I must focus my energy on.

Today, Oliver has just celebrated his first year of working for himself. He successfully overcame his energetic blocks, which allowed him to build momentum towards a more fulfilling future. It wasn't easy. He had to change his lifestyle to free up the energy required to take action on what mattered most. It's still early in this exciting journey of his, but his energetic state is now in a place that whatever the future holds, he is more than ready for it.

When you doubt your power, you give power to your doubt

After I qualified as a certified life coach – a journey that took around two years to complete and hundreds of hours of learning and coaching – I had difficulty doing anything with the qualification. I told those around me that I wasn't feeling fulfilled with my career in finance and that I was doing something about it by looking into starting my own business in something completely different.

Speaking to myself, however, I wasn't so sure.

The path forward was being suffocated by energy blocks that had to be addressed. The thought of giving up the comforts of a decent salary and pension for the uncertainty of income, especially in the short term, filled me with overwhelming unease. I was indecisive as to what choices to make, with my mind tangled up in a mess of overthinking, these words playing on repeat in my mind as each week came and went:

I should spend more time learning how to build a business.

I should meet new people each week and invite them to experience coaching.

I should choose the path that would make me feel most fulfilled.

I should trust myself more and just start before I'm ready.

It sounds so simple now as I write these words to you, but changing that word 'should' to 'must' had a profound impact on my energetic state. It moved me from being paralysed by indecision to empowering me to take action.

'I should trust myself more and just start before I'm ready' became 'I must trust myself more and just start before I'm ready.' Success on our own terms is about choosing 'must' over 'should', because in doing so we speak with greater definiteness of purpose and in the language of an action-oriented person.

Give it a try for yourself:

1. Write down a list of 'should's or 'need's that are currently floating around in your thinking.

2. Replace these words with 'must' or 'will' and notice the difference.
3. If this sparks an idea or a plan in your mind as a result, make sure to note it down and schedule time in your diary to take action on it.

By upgrading the quality of my thinking and words, I began to see myself as a coach, an entrepreneur and the CEO of my life. My identity shifted, and almost automatically so did my behaviour and actions.

It's a powerful demonstration of what we explored in the first part of this book around the activity of visualization. Once you have clarity on who you want to be and what the best version of you looks like, act as if you were already that person. It's a powerful practice when applied. Energetic blocks melt away as your new choices reflect the higher operating frequency of the person that you are transforming into. You disconnect from an identity that no longer serves you and connect to one that drops you back into the river of energetic flow.

Six years after qualifying as a coach, I found myself at the Millennium Gloucester Hotel in London's Kensington for the International Coaching Awards. Staged in the hotel's beautiful palm-tree-adorned conservatory, it was an undoubtedly glamorous event; like being at the Oscars.

As we arrived at the final award of the evening, the tension began to heighten. After the list of nominated individuals was read out along with an overview of their achievements, a golden envelope was opened to reveal the winner.

With my hands clasped together in front of my mouth and my wife's hand on my shoulder, I closed my eyes. As I opened them again, I found myself being showered with coloured confetti and a standing ovation was sweeping across the room and being directed my way.

I had just been named as Life Coach of the Year in front of an audience comprised of my industry peers and colleagues. Hugging my wife, who whispered into my ear how proud she was, I made my way up on to the stage, reflecting on how happy I was that I had chosen a path that would make me feel the most fulfilled and allow me to impact the lives of others in the way that I wanted to.

And in the interviews that I had backstage afterwards, one piece of advice that I shared when asked about my journey was this: 'The more control you have over your mind and awareness of how it influences your reality, the happier you will be. The small steps that you make today to reframe how you perceive yourself and the world around you can be the catalyst for the most wonderful of transformations.'

Be your own placebo

In 2004, Mike Pauletich started experiencing symptoms of what he thought was carpal tunnel syndrome – a condition that causes numbness, tingling or weakness in the hands. His aim with a baseball was off, his arm hurt, his hand shook a little and his wife noticed that he suddenly stopped smiling.

To confirm whether his suspicions were accurate, the forty-two-year-old technology executive booked a visit to his doctor. Following a thorough medical evaluation, however, he discovered that his coordination issues weren't because of his arm or hand but were early signs of Parkinson's disease – a progressive neurological illness caused by a deficiency of the brain neurotransmitter dopamine, with most developing symptoms occurring after the age of fifty. With no known cure available, his doctor told him that within a decade or so there was a very high probability that he wouldn't be able to walk, stand or feed himself. While Pauletich didn't deteriorate as much as had been predicted, he struggled with movement, speaking, writing and depression. It wasn't looking good, and he became desperate to explore experimental treatments in the small hope that they could help him get better.

In 2011, he came across news of a Parkinson's study being conducted by the company Ceregene. They were in the process of testing a novel gene therapy that sounded aggressive: the procedure involved the drilling of two small holes in the patient's skull, followed by the injection of the protein neurturin directly into specific regions of the brain. It had been shown in monkeys that injections of this protein could alleviate the progress of the disease by protecting and even possibly repairing damaged dopamine-secreting neurons. Despite testing on humans being at such an early stage, he was willing to enrol in the study to give it a try. He had a belief that undergoing this brain surgery would help him fight the disease once and for all.

The result? Nothing short of an absolute miracle.

Prior to the surgery he found it painful to move around and had to explain to clients of his company that his slurred speech wasn't caused by excessive drinking. After coming out from surgery, his shaking vanished, his mobility significantly improved and he spoke articulately. It got to a point where it was difficult to tell whether he had any symptoms at all. His physician on the study, Stanford neurologist Dr Kathleen Poston, was astonished by these results. The disease had never before been reversed in humans. The best hope was for a slowdown in the progression of the disease, and even this was extremely rare.

Then in April 2013, the final results of Ceregene's study were released: it had failed.

There were no significant improvements in symptoms related to Parkinson's disease for the patients who received the injection of neurturin versus the control group who had received a placebo treatment – those in this latter group had the small holes cut in their skulls to make it feel as if there had been an operation, but in reality no neurturin at all was injected. The results both surprised and disappointed Dr Poston.

However, after looking closer into the study's data, she was shocked to learn that Pauletich was in the group that didn't receive any neurturin. He got the placebo instead. Remembering her patient's miraculous improvement, she wondered how this could be when no treatment was received.

Pauletich's recovery illustrates just how powerful the placebo effect can be on us. Flooding our mind with high expectations is what drives the placebo effect – a belief that becomes so potent that it has this extraordinary ability to heal. When story and imagination are in sync together like a flawless symphony, the results can be astounding.

Within the field of medicine, science shows that this placebo effect can trigger a neurochemical response through the release of endorphins or opium-like painkillers from the brain that intercepts and inhibits pain. In Pauletich's case, the mind instructed his body to get better but in order for this to take form, he had to be convinced that change was about to occur when he signed up to the Ceregene study. It's through the anticipation of recovery that our minds take on a role similar to that of a pharmacist, prescribing us with the medicine that we seek to heal us.

If the placebo effect proves anything, it is that you must never underestimate the influence that your energetic state can have on your wellbeing. Your thoughts can make you feel ill and stressed or excited and energized; it is the key that ignites the engine of healing and is a testament to the immense power of the human mind.

We are born with this extraordinary capacity to create energetic shifts in our reality, and to become our own placebo is to be conscious about our thoughts and what we choose to believe in, because it is in our thinking that our customized human experience of life is created. Reality is nothing more than perception, and your perception of the world is determined by your energetic state. Transform your energy and you transform your life.

Awareness around the nature of thought equips you with the ability to bend your reality and shape your experiences towards a more desirable outcome. Thoughts are just thoughts – at any given moment you can choose one over another – and those that you believe to be true will manifest themselves into your reality. Your mind, therefore, is the birthplace of every victory and every defeat. Bend your reality to one that is aligned to your highest values and it will fill you with the energy to fulfil your potential instead of one that blocks your progress and keeps you playing small.

One of the activities that I get my clients to play with to demonstrate how they can become their own placebo is that of daily affirmations, which are positive, empowering and spoken out loud in the present tense as if they were an undeniable fact. They not only help to programme your mind for happiness and success by tattooing clusters of positively charged thoughts on to your brain, but they help to raise your energetic frequency.

During his professional boxing career, Muhammad Ali didn't say to himself and others that he could be the greatest or that he wished he could be as good as one of his competitors. Instead, he constantly repeated to himself and anybody that would listen the following words: 'I am the greatest.' He believed it even before reaching the levels of success that he did, and in the process he convinced himself and everyone around him that he was already a champion. 'It's the repetition of affirmations that leads to belief,' said Ali in his book *The Greatest: My Own Story.* 'And once that belief becomes a deep conviction, things begin to happen.'

Here are a few examples of powerful affirmations that you can begin practising each day:

- Life is always happening for me.
- I am enough.
- The universe provides me with everything I need to become who I am meant to be.
- I have a natural flow of creative energy that will lead me to the answers I seek.
- I am a money magnet.
- My life is just getting started.
- I am an energetic force of nature and anything is possible for me.

The affirmation that I repeat most often is this: 'Life is always happening for me.' Not only does it keep me in the feeling of flow, but it also shifts my energy towards the extraordinary. With energetic blocks removed, I'm living as if success is inevitable and as if it's impossible to fail. I am tapping into the essence of pronoia – a word that means the exact opposite of paranoia. It is the belief that the universe is secretly conspiring in your favour, that life is working for you (not against you) and that something good is always going to happen.

By believing in and being emotionally connected to a thought that may currently exist only in your mind, your heightened mental state uplifts your physiology and energy to turn the invisible into the visible. And since your mind is like a supercomputer designing your reality in this present moment, you must learn how to operate it well. As you do so, the benefits to you will be nothing short of transformational.

5
Turn Obstacles into a Source of Energy

'And once the storm is over, you won't remember how you made it through, how you managed to survive. You won't even be sure whether the storm is really over. But one thing is certain. When you come out of the storm, you won't be the same person who walked in. That's what this storm's all about.'

HARUKI MURAKAMI

There's this Taoist story of an old farmer who had worked his crops for many years. One day his horse ran away. Upon hearing the news, his neighbours came around to commiserate with him. 'We're sorry to hear that your beloved horse ran away. Such terrible luck,' they said sympathetically. The farmer replied, 'Maybe, maybe not.'

The next morning, the horse returned home bringing with it three wild horses. 'How wonderful! Not only has your horse returned, but you now have more horses,' exclaimed the neighbours. 'Maybe, maybe not,' replied the farmer.

The following day, the farmer's son attempted to ride one of the untamed horses when he was suddenly thrown on to the ground, breaking his leg during the fall. The neighbours again came to offer their sympathy for his misfortune. 'What terrible luck,' they said. 'Maybe, maybe not,' replied the farmer.

The day after, military officials marched through the village to draft young men into the army. Seeing that the old farmer's son had a broken leg, they passed him by. The neighbours congratulated the farmer on how well things had turned out and commented on how lucky they were. To which the farmer again replied, 'Maybe, maybe not.'

Many of us are like the neighbours in this story. We're quick to judge, and we waste our energy dwelling on and worrying about that which we can't control. Life is constantly surprising us with obstacles and when you focus on what you can't control, you become easily paralysed by overthinking and negativity. When you focus on what you can control, you feel energized and become empowered to take action.

Imagine, however, if you were to approach unexpected events in life with a similar mindset to that of the old farmer? To be attached to no outcome and open to everything – to pause, reflect and have the humility to seek the lessons in the many challenges that you will encounter. 'To do anything extraordinary,' noted author and podcast host Srinivas Rao, 'you must accept the duality that nothing is guaranteed and anything is possible.' And as our story illustrates, perception matters: you get to choose the meaning that you give to the events you experience and it's this that determines how you show up in the world.

Perspective is everything, and adopting the lens of optimism can empower you when faced with obstacles, equipping you with the vision and wisdom to take positive action around that which is in your control. A couple of questions that I tend to reflect on whenever I encounter setbacks so that I can turn them into a source of energy are:

1. What else could this mean?
2. What is the lesson here?
3. What could I do differently if this were to happen again?

The truth is that for every challenge you face, there's often a hidden blessing in disguise. Even more so when you operate from the belief that life is always working for you rather than against you.

Just like the stock market, progress in life is rarely ever a straight line. The way that I like to think of it is that life is less a sprint or a marathon, and more like navigating your way through a great big maze. There will be dead ends, moments where you have to start again, days when you simply have to pause to reflect on the best way forward, and periods where you're in energetic flow.

Ultimately, life isn't about what happens to you, it's about how you choose to respond to what happens to you, because it is in this response where your greatest power lies.

Think about it for a moment – much about happiness is the result of how you choose to respond to the things that are outside your control. Two people with the same circumstances can have very different experiences simply because of how they choose to interpret and respond to them.

The adventure is always in the journey, and the stories that are born as a result of us taking up that call to create a more fulfilling life are what shape us into who we become. And these stories of yours? They will become your legacy – they will energize and inspire others to walk their own path and to

What we think the path of life looks like

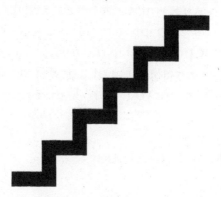

What the path of life actually looks like

see that within every obstacle lies an abundance of opportunity. Never underestimate the impact that your courage and strength can have on others.

Take a moment to reflect on those obstacles that you may currently be facing. What if they're not meant to paralyse you but to serve as a source of energy for your growth? And as for it being bad luck, in the words of that old farmer: maybe, maybe not.

While your life won't always go to plan, it can often end up being exactly what you need, because challenges help you to improve and develop into a better version of yourself, and this gift can come presented in the form of a lesson, a timely redirection or the development of a new skill. And the greater the challenge, the more you get to learn about yourself.

Failure is your rocket fuel

'What did you fail at this week?'

This is the question that a young Sara Blakely was asked by her father at the dinner table at the end of each week. It was an interesting experience for her. When she didn't have something she had failed at that week to share, he would be disappointed; when she did, he would give her a high-five. Her father showed her that not only was she still loved after failing, she was celebrated for it.

She didn't realize it at the time, but what her father was doing was reframing her definition and understanding of failure. In an interview with *Fortune*, she highlights that 'My dad taught me that failing simply just leads you to the next great thing.' For Blakely, failure evolved into less of an outcome and became more about not trying.

What will you fail at this week?

Many people don't try because they're too afraid to fail, but once you realize that the only real failure is in never trying, the universe opens up to you in ways that force your mind to completely reimagine what is possible – that an extraordinary life awaits when you are willing to let go of the ordinary.

This shift in her energetic state was the foundation for

Blakely to eventually go on to become named by *Forbes* as the youngest self-made female billionaire in the world through the launch and success of her company Spanx, founded during her late twenties. It gave her the energy to take risks, to constantly expand her comfort zone and to try.

Let's get this out of the way just so that we're clear: no one is perfect.

Not you, not me and not any of the people that you look up to in life. We're all human and that means that failure is a part of our lives. Even more so when you have made the conscious decision to set sail beyond the lines drawn by your comfort zone and to dismantle the energetic blocks that have held you back. However, failure can act as rocket fuel for your growth in the same way it has for Blakely. And when you look back, you won't see them as failures; you will remember them as moments that have contributed to your resilience and comebackability. Moments that have energized your life to take an unexpected turn for the better and helped you find peace in allowing yourself to be perfectly imperfect.

Too many of us grow up being taught how success and failure are opposites: you either succeed or you fail. And this often continues into the world of work, where an exclusively performance-driven culture can result in employees being afraid to experiment with new ideas for fear of them not working out. It negatively influences our energetic state and holds us back from fully expressing ourselves. Your energy is suppressed, which leads to feelings of disengagement.

Some kind of failure always happens before success, and if you have a poor relationship with failure, you can't possibly do what must be done to make meaningful progress. As the popular saying goes, 'The difference between a master and a

What people see

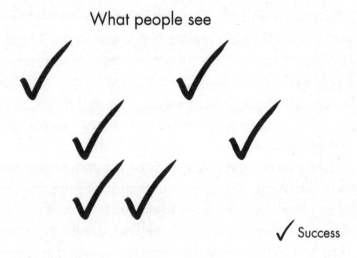

✓ Success

What people don't see

✕ Failure

beginner is that the master has failed more times than the beginner has even tried.'

This is what Jeff Bezos wrote in his 2015 letter to Amazon shareholders, communicating the importance of experimenting and how innovation is born from a willingness to fail:

One area where I think we are especially distinctive is failure. I believe we are the best place in the world to fail (we have plenty of practice!), and failure and invention are inseparable twins.

To invent you have to experiment, and, if you know in advance that it's going to work, it's not an experiment.

Most large organizations embrace the idea of invention, but are not willing to suffer the string of failed experiments necessary to get there. Outsized returns often come from betting against conventional wisdom, and conventional wisdom is unusually right.

Given a 10% chance of a 100 times payoff, you should take that bet every time. But you're still going to be wrong nine times out of ten.

The world's most successful people aren't afraid of failure. They embrace it, learn from it and use it as fuel to energize them forward. They know that you can't play it safe your whole life and expect to get close to what you're capable of. With every failure, you learn something new. Failure is your rocket fuel – a wise teacher disguised in the form of an event – and it shows you the way by showing you what isn't.

If you want to step out from being a supporting character of your story and into the arena of being the hero of it, you must transform failure into a guide – a guide that you can learn from and use as a platform to that next level of your life. If you're thinking that failure hurts, you're not alone. It can hurt like hell if you don't know how to turn it into a source of energy to help you come back stronger.

When I'm asked about how I respond to failure at events I'm invited to speak at, I often share an approach that I call

RISE (Reframe the setback, Immerse yourself in inspiration, Self-compassion and Energy switching).

1. Reframe the setback

Fear of failure can stop so many of us taking action, but what is failure really? When you think about it objectively, it's nothing more than feedback, an education and a step to something better. A simple reframe like this, therefore, can help you to see failure from a more productive perspective and to appreciate that you always learn more from what goes wrong than from what goes right. Seen in this way, failure becomes an experience that develops your resilience and confidence, elevates your energetic state and acts as a catalyst for transformation.

Ego sees failure. Humility sees feedback.
Ego seeks perfection. Humility seeks progress.
Ego blames. Humility learns.

The universe will deliver moments of beauty, opportunity and pain to your doorstep. One of the greatest insights that you will come to experience is that all of these are sources of energy, if you are humble enough to seek the lessons contained within each.

2. Immerse yourself in inspiration

When faced with failure, which comes in all shapes and sizes, this strategy helps to feed your comebackability. You may have missed out on a promotion, lost someone important or had to shut down a business venture. Coming back stronger from events like this isn't always straightforward, but when you immerse yourself in inspiration you find the energy not to let failure defeat you, because inspiration is a force that breathes energy into you, compelling you to take action.

It's why I love reading and watching great stories. Learning from someone who has come up against obstacles, failed in their efforts, learnt from the setback and then undergone a transformation to come back stronger than ever before gives me the energy to go out and do the same. It's the feeling I got when I first came across Nick Vujicic, for example, who was born with tetra-amelia syndrome – a rare disorder character-ized by the absence of arms and legs. His mother refused to see or hold him when he was first presented to her by the nurse. Despite these challenges, he went on to launch an inter-national non-profit organization, publish multiple books and start a family with his wife – they now have four children.

3. Self-compassion

It's important for you to understand that failing does not make you a failure. Failure is an event, not an identity state-ment. If you've failed at something, remind yourself that you can't learn to stand up without falling or improve without critical feedback. The experience may not be fun in the moment, but it's a valuable part of any personal growth jour-ney. Be kind and forgive yourself when you make mistakes. You're only human, and you must balance these inevitable events with an appreciation of just how far you have come in order to be where you are today.

The success that you seek is often born out of a series of failures, so when you avoid taking action because you're afraid of making mistakes or being judged by others, you block your chances for success. Be proud of your failures along the way and take more risks – it will be thanks to these so-called failures that you come to know what you know. If you don't, you will never truly succeed or achieve anything worthwhile, because the path of least resistance is rarely the path towards a meaningful life. It's the path of resistance that fuels your growth and helps you to become the person who can achieve more in life.

4. Energy switching

Put simply, this is about switching your energy from negative to positive actions. Negative actions are unproductive and include things such as endlessly replaying the event in your head and finding someone or something to pin the blame on. These are energetic blocks to your flow. Positive actions, on the other hand, are productive and keep you focused on making progress. These include activities that help you clear your mind (exercise, journalling, meditation) and remind you of the vision you're working towards.

The late Kobe Bryant is widely regarded as one of the greatest basketball players of all time, but what few are aware of is that he also missed more shots than any other player: 14,481 to be precise. And this is exactly what made him a great. He confronted failure game after game, shooting and missing, shooting and missing, until he had shot and missed more than any other man ever to play in the league. Over time, he got comfortable with the idea of failure and was willing to dance with it in every game he played. If someone is better than you at something, it is very likely that they have failed at it more times than you have, because it is through those failures that talent and mastery are developed.

Life doesn't get any easier or more forgiving. You just get

stronger and more resilient each time you dust yourself down, get back up and stand tall in the face of failure with faith in your ability to move forward.

Having the wisdom to learn from your mistakes can catapult you from victim to victor and from helpless to hopeful. As the actor Sylvester Stallone said in his 2006 film *Rocky Balboa*: 'You, me, or nobody is gonna hit as hard as life. But it ain't about how hard you hit. It's about how hard you can get hit and keep moving forward; how much you can take and keep moving forward. That's how winning is done.'

Winners don't blame. Winners take responsibility.

Winners don't give up. Winners come back stronger.

Winners don't complain. Winners take control.

Don't let failure define you. Instead, let it act as rocket fuel towards unleashing your genius and your extraordinary.

Life is a journey of discovery and, to progress, you must make the ascent up your own mountains. Climbing any mountain is no easy task. It will be a rocky ride: there will be rivers of change that you must swim through and storms that will test how much you want what you say you want. It's easy to play it safe and avoid taking any risks in life. But that isn't living; it's a sure path to a life full of regrets. When you channel your energy into the path that will teach you the most, however, you will experience the purpose of life: to live with purpose, to fulfil your potential and to share your talent with the world.

Flowing with the energy of purpose, possibilities and persistence, you don't care how many times you fail because you have this deep sense of knowing that you will eventually succeed, and that failure is simply life's way of redirecting you towards something better.

Adapt to thrive

According to legend, wing chun – a Chinese martial art and form of self-defence – was first created by Buddhist nun Ng Mui, who was a master of Shaolin kung fu. Drawing on her training and personal experiences, she designed a compact version of kung fu to exploit weaknesses inherent in the other combat styles of her time and give an advantage to smaller fighters like herself. This new system was well guarded and passed on to just a few dedicated students. Her style soon became known as wing chun, after her first student and protégé, a woman named Yim Wing Chun.

As a teenager, Yim Wing Chun had fallen in love with Leung Bok Chau. Before they could get married, however, she caught the eye of a local warlord who pursued her to be his own wife instead. His many advances were rebuffed, until an offer was made that would allow her to move on with her life: he would rescind his proposal for marriage if she could beat him in a fight, one-on-one. She agreed, and after her father negotiated for time in order for her to train for this, the warlord gave her until the following spring to prepare. He didn't think it would make any difference and so he began the preparations for her to become his bride.

News of her predicament and the scheduled fight quickly spread throughout the small village, and soon she was approached by an older woman whom she had befriended at a tofu shop. This woman was Ng Mui, who revealed that she was one of the Shaolin Five Elders who had managed to escape the burning of their temple. She knew that tiny young Yim Wing Chun was no match for the fierce warlord, whose strength was unequalled.

Ng Mui, however, had a plan in mind.

The new fighting system that she had been working on was designed to better suit a woman or other fighter who did not possess the advantage of size and strength. She had adapted kung fu to help women overcome what they lacked, and she began at once to train Yim Wing Chun in this new style, concentrating solely on the most essential elements that could be absorbed and applied in just a few months instead of a few years.

By the following spring, when the warlord returned to claim his bride, Yim Wing Chun was ready.

In front of the entire village, she demonstrated a version of kung fu that had never been seen before. She used the warlord's mass and strength against him, flowing effortlessly around and under his attempts to strike or grab her. Despite a weight difference of nearly a hundred pounds, she directed her entire body weight and energy towards specific targets that broke the warlord's balance and left him vulnerable to repeated strikes. When the warlord collapsed in front of her feet after being knocked unconscious, roars and cheers swept across the crowd, who were left stunned by what they had just witnessed. A legend had just been born.

Yim Wing Chun may have lacked the size and strength that the warlord possessed, but her ability to adapt through Ng Mui's teachings allowed her to overcome this obstacle. When faced with obstacles, we can choose to be defeated by them or respond with creativity and resourcefulness. We must adapt and innovate, because, as Louisiana professor of business management Leon Megginson noted, 'It is not the strongest of the species that survives, nor the most intelligent, but the one most adaptable to change.' With life changing at a faster rate than ever before, we must be in a constant state of adaptation if we want to succeed and thrive – to unlearn what no longer serves us so that we may create the space to learn what does. To disrupt ourselves so that we may surf the waves of change and uncertainty more eloquently. Instead of fighting against obstacles, we embrace them and adapt in the same way that Yim Wing Chun did in overcoming that which she lacked. It is how resilience is built.

The challenges that you have overcome in the past also act as important reminders of just how far you have come since then. Without them, you wouldn't have the opportunity to evolve to that next level. See challenges therefore as fuel for your growth instead of something to fear and avoid – use them to push you creatively instead of letting them defeat you.

When the coronavirus pandemic swept across the planet in 2020, it wrought havoc on the lives of many – from losing loved ones and not being able to attend their funerals to losing jobs as industries either restructured or faced closure. One of those affected was my client Maria, who had spent years developing her career as a teacher only to be faced with redundancy as the realities of living in a global pandemic set in.

During our first meeting, it was clear that she was drowning in overthinking, worrying about how she was going to land another job in what was a very difficult time for everyone.

After doing some breathing exercises to calm her mind and ground her in the present moment, I got her to do the following exercise as a way to refocus, which I also invite you to do if you're currently dealing with a challenge in an area of your life:

1. Write down a brief outline of the challenge that you
   are currently facing. In Maria's case, it was: 'I will no
   longer be in my current job and must work out a
   plan for the best way forward from here.'

2. Make a list of what you can't control.

3. Make a list of what you can control.

4. Reflect on which of these lists you are currently spending most of your energy on, and the impact it has on your energetic state. What else did you notice while putting the lists together?

5. Decide today to take responsibility for where you are and to let go of that which you can't control. If it helps, put a line through the things that you can't control. Now imagine what it would look like when your energy is now exclusively focused on the things you can control.

6. Looking through the list of what you can control, break these down into some small action steps and highlight one that you can commit to following through with this week.

The visual on the following page shows some of what Maria wrote down.

The first thing she noticed was just how much of her time was spent dwelling on the things that were outside her control. It was unproductive and a waste of her time and energy. By shifting her focus to that which was more within her control, we were able to start mapping out an exciting plan that took into consideration her values and what she ultimately wanted to achieve in life. Breaking these down into smaller action steps that she could follow through with ahead of our next meeting, she now had something to channel her energy into. Within just a few months, she was making giant leaps forward. She had finished recording two online courses on subjects that she had years of experience in, uploaded them on to a virtual learning platform and successfully enrolled her first

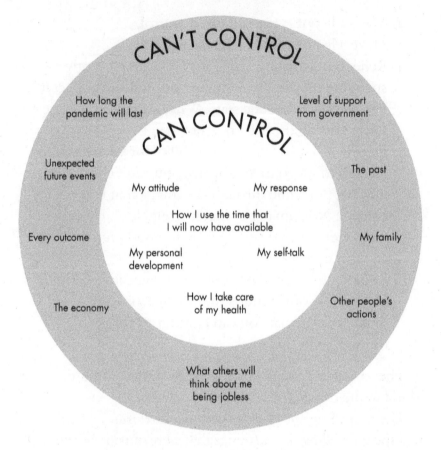

250 students. The experience inspired her to pursue other exciting projects, and she now looks back on the day that she was made redundant as a blessing, calling this new phase of her life 'a rebirth'.

If you want to live the life that you desire, you can't expect it to arrive smoothly. It almost never does. The reality is that creating a successful life, career or business around your greatest passions is going to be challenging. There will be moments when you will want to give up and return to the cosiness of your comfort zone. When you persist regardless of how many times you fall, however, you will evolve and grow.

You are asked to become more than you were, and this means developing new perspectives, acquiring new skills and finding the energy to push beyond boundaries.

Life is too short to waste your limited mental energy on worrying about events that are outside your control. Instead, I hope you take ownership of and action on the things that you can control. I hope you are open enough to adapt and embrace challenges as a source of energy. Because the greatest reward from overcoming challenges in life is knowing that you are someone who can overcome challenges in life. This realization and shift in identity is monumental and life-changing.

6
Make Momentum Your Friend

*'There is no perfect moment. No time when you will know
enough to guarantee you will get what you want. No time you'll
be 100% sure that you're ready to have a child, fall in love, take
a job, move cross-country, build a business, show your work,
stand in your truth, pursue your dreams.'*

JONATHAN FIELDS

The two event organizers approached me at the front of the
room to confirm if I was ready to start in fifteen minutes. I
was about to deliver a presentation to a room of over sixty
people curious about what I had to say; ambitious individuals
who were working their way up the corporate ladder, many
of whom were also responsible for leading teams of employees beneath them.

They didn't know it at the time, but I was a public-speaking
virgin.

This was my first taste of being paid to deliver a presentation – and talk about jumping in right at the deep end by accepting an invitation from a multinational corporation that had a presence in over forty countries worldwide! Because a few of my mentors had advised me to begin before I was ready, I had decided to grab this paid opportunity with both hands and to figure out later how I was going to give them a good return on their investment.

I had no experience of any sort of formal speaker training, and while I may have delivered a talk just a couple of months prior, it was more as a favour for a good friend who ran a small community of aspiring entrepreneurs, and only four people decided to show up. This was despite being told that there were twenty people who had registered to attend. Maybe the no-shows were sceptical about what they could learn from a Chinese thirty-something who looked like he could be an enforcer for a triad gang. It felt less like I was delivering a presentation and more like I was sharing my story as part of an Alcoholics Anonymous group meeting. I was praying that this corporate event wasn't going to have as many no-shows.

As I turned to the organizers to reassure them that I was all good to go, I suddenly realized that my extensively prepared notes weren't with me.

The idea was to lay these sheets of paper across the keyboard of my laptop to help guide me through the ninety minutes that I would be speaking. They had the exercises that I planned to get the participants to do, the statistics that I wanted to highlight and the prompts on stories I wanted to share. I desperately scrambled through my belongings to find them before resigning myself to the fact that I must've forgotten them in my rush to get here on time.

Excusing myself from the room for a few minutes, I sprinted towards the toilets at a speed an Olympic athlete would be proud of. Locking myself in one of the cubicles, I punched the wall in frustration, berating myself at how I could've left something so important, that I had spent the last few weeks putting together, at home. As I sat down, I noticed drops of red blood hitting the floor and immediately turned to grab some toilet paper to stem the flow from my nose.

'What a moment to get a nosebleed,' I thought.

My nose and warmer temperatures have never got on well together, but this was a cold, dark evening. I mean, it was even snowing outside. With just minutes to go before I was to be introduced as the evening's entertainment, and determined not to let this nosebleed checkmate me, I stood up tall and straight, shoved some tissue up my right nostril, centred my attention on my breathing and visualized this event being a roaring success. It was time to trust in my power and to simply focus on giving it my best shot.

Ninety minutes later and in need of plenty of water, I had just survived my first event as a paid public speaker. In the process, I had learnt to trust and believe in myself more – something that can so often prove a high hurdle to overcome for many taking those first steps into the discomfort of the unknown. It also taught me that in order to master something new, we must be willing to regularly throw ourselves directly into situations such as these that result in pain and growth. It requires us to begin before we think we're ready, because doing the things that scare us is what helps to build our confidence and energy through the accumulation of small yet important wins.

When I arrived home, my girlfriend asked how it went, and I told her that the feeling was similar to that of finishing one of those fitness bootcamp classes we attended each week: half of me felt glad that it was over and half of me couldn't wait to return to do it all again.

As I made my way to the shower, she said, 'I hope you got those notes that you left on the hallway table OK. I took photos of them and sent them to your phone while you were on your way to the venue.'

Taking out my phone, I realized I still had it on flight mode, and, after turning that off, I saw the images come flooding through in my notifications. Not only that, but there was a message from my contact at the company that I had just spoken at. She told me that the feedback was very positive and asked if we could schedule a call for later in the month to explore other ways of working together. Before she signed off on the message, she noted that, 'Your energy was infectious and just what we needed at this time of year.' And just like that, my public-speaking journey had officially begun.

The experience taught me that if you don't do things that are scary, you won't have the opportunity to build your confidence, and confidence is the reward you get when you succeed despite your fears. And as for my energy being infectious? I feel that it was the result of being completely in the present moment with the audience, the excitement of stretching myself and trusting in my power. By letting go of everything out of my control, I was able to fully express myself and share my energy with the room.

Old maps won't get you to new destinations

Realizing what you want isn't too hard; acting upon it, however, will be one of your greatest challenges and will demonstrate to the world what you really believe in. You need more energy to get going for sure, but once you're in motion, you need less to keep moving forward. It's like a rocket launching from earth into space: you need a lot of energy to get it out of the earth's atmosphere and to overcome the pull of gravity. Except for us, it's not the pull of gravity holding us back, but the pull of our comfort zones.

Here's a question for you: when was the last time you did something for the first time that stretched you out of your comfort zone?

The response for too many of us is years, if not decades, and an awareness of this should act as a catalyst for us to take action.

We can spend far too long living life on autopilot and rooted deep down into the soil of our comfort zones. Comfort, however, is the enemy of progress; it's only when you set sail beyond the edges of your map that the energy of possibilities can begin to appear. Old maps certainly won't get you to new destinations.

Yes, being in your comfort zone may feel nice and cosy, but if you're not careful it will lead to mediocrity and a lack of fulfilment.

'Inaction breeds doubt and fear,' noted Dale Carnegie, adding that 'action breeds confidence and courage. If you want to conquer fear, do not sit at home and think about it. Go out and get busy.' To live fully, you must be willing to step outside that safe space you have created for yourself. Too often, we find it tough to say goodbye to the things that make us miserable because they also make us comfortable. You must not lose your sense of adventure; once you are firmly rooted in what is comfortable, everything else will become too risky: changing jobs, learning a new skill or following your heart.

The action that you take today builds your experience, that experience builds your confidence, and that confidence builds momentum.

Don't be that person who spends their energy just talking about their ideas. Instead, be that person who invests their energy into the execution of those ideas. While the rewards of seeing any idea come to life are exciting, real happiness comes from the feeling of progress and the personal growth that you will experience. We must therefore channel our energy into what we can do today, right now.

No one can predict with full certainty where the world will be a few weeks from today, let alone a few years from today. What we know for sure, though, is that by taking purposeful action in this present moment, you are proactively contributing to a better future for yourself. This is what it means by focusing on and enjoying the process.

Take a moment now to pause and write down your thoughts in response to the following questions:

1. If, in one year's time, you are still exactly where you are now, how would that make you feel?
2. Now, imagine where you could be a year from today if instead of avoiding those things that you know you must do, you actually did them every day?

One tiny step forward each day snowballs into at least 365 steps forward in a year's time. Having a strong bias to action is what separates the most successful from the rest, because it is this that turns the impossible into the possible, and the possible into the inevitable. Don't wait for anyone to give you permission to begin. You qualify yourself by simply showing up and doing the work. As Steve Jobs shared during a speech in 1994: 'Most people never pick up the phone. Most people never call and ask. And that's what separates sometimes the people who do things from those who just dream about them. You gotta act.'

Enthusiasm, ideas and talk are common; commitment, execution and consistency are rare.

The trap that most people fall into is this idea that we have to have it all figured out and we must've reached this mythical point of readiness before we can take that first step forward. Don't be like most people. Rid your mind of this thinking, because nobody really has it all figured out. Everyone is figuring it out as they go along, just like you. Action is the path that gets you from ambiguity to clarity, and there's nothing quite like being reminded of just how short life is to spur you into taking action. The image on the following page is pinned up to be that constant reminder to me.

It tells you how old I currently am at the time of writing this book and how ambitious I am in wanting to live until at least 100 years old. The fact that not all of us get to that age just adds another layer of motivation to make the most of the years that we have available.

The truth is that you must begin before you are ready, otherwise you will be waiting a very long time to take those first steps. And the longer you wait to do something that you know deep down you must do now, the greater the odds are that you will never actually do it. Tomorrow becomes next week, next week becomes next month and next month becomes next year. Next year may even become never. Writing

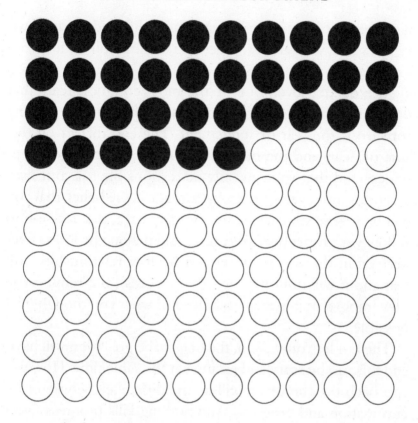

Visual of a 100-year life in years (current age = 36)

in her third diary, published in 1966, French-born novelist Anaïs Nin noted that 'Life shrinks or expands in proportion to one's courage.' You will always be afraid and you will never be 100% ready, which is exactly why you must begin today. Excuses will always be there for you, opportunity will not.

And when I speak about courage, it doesn't mean that we don't harbour any fears. Fear is the price of admission to doing all that makes us feel most alive, and to live in the fire of aliveness is the best form of living. Fear will always be a passenger in our lives seeking to keep us safe from danger. However, we must not let it jump into the driving seat, because it can easily trick us into living a boring life and going down to our grave with all our hopes and dreams still buried deep inside.

At a deeper level, one of the most common fears that drains our precious energy reserves and prevents us moving forward is the fear of judgement. The ego thrives on this sort of fear, and the only way to put it out of a job is to understand that you can only be responsible for your own reactions, not everyone else's. Courage is the belief that you will be OK despite the fears you may have, the decision to follow your heart over your fears and making progress over perfection the focus. Develop a healthy relationship with fear and it will not only fuel your progress, but remind you how important it is to stretch beyond what you thought was possible.

The bolder your vision, the bigger the goals you will have, and this can be scary and exciting at the same time. How you approach this, however, will be the difference between procrastination and progress. And nothing kills progress faster than indecision. To avoid the overwhelm that can be experienced when pursuing big goals, the key is to break them down into smaller steps and tiny bite-size actions so that the path ahead doesn't feel as daunting. Start where you are, get some small wins under your belt, and it will give you the energy to continue moving forward.

Criticizing and pointing your finger at others while sitting on the sidelines is easy. Having the courage to take action on what is most important and daring to take that leap of faith into a future populated with unknowns, now that is harder to do. It's why you must have a vision of what success means to you, because those who do the work are more interested in their future than in their past. And the truth is that you will rarely be criticized by someone who is doing more than you, for they are far too busy taking action themselves on their own compelling vision to waste time judging others.

There is this fine line between wanting to do something and deciding to do it, and the side that you fall into will influence the intensity of your actions. Many of us don't trust ourselves enough to take a step into the abyss of the unknown. But everything in life is unknown until you try. Don't be afraid to be seen as starting as a beginner; every success story was a beginner once. And don't let overthinking and inaction kill those great ideas and opportunities of yours. The biggest mistake that you can make is to think that you have forever when you don't. Life is happening right now. And if you delay doing the things that energize you, you will never get to experience what life could've looked like with your wings spread. Right now might just be the best chance you have to take action, because the secret to getting ahead and to feeling fulfilled is to simply get started. Knowledge may come from learning and exercising your curiosity, but transformation can only occur from the application of that knowledge.

Focus your energy, therefore, less on what you have to lose and what could go wrong, and more towards what you stand to gain and what could go right. Because the world needs that unique energy that only you can bring to what you are most passionate about. It needs you to be you.

After all, would you rather look back to today in five years' time and say 'I wish I had', or 'I'm so glad that I did'? Every day that you wait is another day you will never get back. If you want to start changing your future, you must quit waiting for the right time and be willing to cross that starting line. Be bold, be brave and take those first steps over the edges and corners of your map, because success won't come looking for you while you wait around thinking about being ready to take action. To live is to channel your energy into creation; what will you focus your energy on creating in this lifetime of yours?

Interested or committed?

During an interview that I did with the BBC before the beginning of another New Year, I was asked by the host about why so many people who make resolutions at the start of the year break them so quickly or simply fail to follow through with what they told themselves they were going to do.

The short answer I said was not to make New Year resolutions. We shouldn't have to wait until the beginning of a new year to make positive changes in our lives. It's like saying that you're finally going to start something once you've achieved that promotion, landed that next client or saved enough money. This isn't a very good mindset to have. Personal development must be something you embrace on a daily basis.

The longer answer was down to the difference between being 'interested' and being 'committed'. Resolutions tend to be vague in nature and, as a result, not very motivating. We find ourselves only interested in creating a plan around them and don't have any sense of urgency to take action. A real decision, however, involves risk, uncertainty and commitment. When this occurs, the path ahead emerges because, as the Zen proverb highlights so eloquently, 'When the student is ready, the teacher will appear.'

Interest is 50/50; you haven't decided.
Commitment is 100% invested in a decision.

Interest is worried about a lack of resources.
Commitment is excited by resourcefulness.

Interest says 'I should' and 'I might'.
Commitment says 'I must' and 'I will'.

Interest is focused on what could go wrong.
Commitment is focused on what could go right.

Interest waits until the New Year to make changes.
Commitment begins today to make changes.

Interest takes action once in a while when time allows and the feeling is right.
Commitment makes time to take action on a consistent basis.

Interest loves distraction.
Commitment loves progress.

Look at where you are right now. This is what you are telling the world that you are committed to. If you want things to be different, you must commit to that difference. 'At the moment of commitment,' noted Johann Wolfgang von Goethe, 'the entire universe conspires to assist you.' It is in your moment of commitment that you spark a shift in the universe around you as it hears your call and your desire to step up.

When you commit, your mind shifts away from indecision to thoughts of 'how' and 'who'.

'How can I make best use of my time this week to move forward in this area?'

'Who can help me in achieving this goal that I have set for myself?'

And the fastest way to move from interest to commitment is to know why what you want matters. Put simply, the more reasons you have and the more emotionally connected you are to it, the easier it becomes to 'see' the best way forward. If you don't know why you're doing something, it's difficult to sustain your focus, energy and discipline in the face of an avalanche of distractions.

This is a great exercise to help you get to the root cause of why something matters, which elevates the level of your commitment. I will share an example of how a client may answer these questions and I suggest you follow along using your own responses for reference:

Q1. What is important to you about the vision that you shared with me?

A1. I want to be able to look forward to each week with excitement rather than dread.

You: _____
_____
_____

Q2: What is important to you about being able to look forward to each week with excitement rather than dread?

A2: Because at the moment, I feel like I'm wasting my life away by doing something that isn't making me happy or bringing me joy.

You: _____

_____

_____

Q3: What is important about doing something that makes you happy and brings you joy?

A3: I will be able to show up better each day and be able to contribute more by having a role that allows me to express the strengths that come naturally to me.

You: _____

_____

_____

Q4: What is important about having a role that allows you to express the strengths that come naturally to you?

A4: It will make me feel more fulfilled knowing that I have value that I can bring to this world through the work that I do. Creating the lifestyle I desire by doing the work I am passionate about and positively impacting the lives of others will be incredible.

You: _____

_____

_____

Q5: What is important about bringing value to this world and positively impacting the lives of others?

A5: I want to leave a real legacy and to live a story that will inspire others to do the same, especially my two young children. I want people to remember how I made the world better in my own small way.

You: _____

_____

_____

Our reasons often start at a superficial level, but as we dig deeper layer by layer, we heighten our motivation. And when it moves our heart, we discover the courage within to turn our thoughts into action and to share our gifts with the world.

When you are truly committed, you will make that first move. American philosopher and ethnobotanist Terence McKenna said: 'Nature loves courage. You make the commitment and nature will respond to that commitment by removing impossible obstacles. Dream the impossible dream and the world will not grind you under, it will lift you up. This is the trick. This is what all these teachers and philosophers who really counted, who really touched the alchemical gold, this is what they understood.' Your commitment becomes a reflection of your desires because when you really want something, you commit to that thing.

You find a way to make it happen, you get laser-focused and you harness the power of audacity. And audacity is all about having the energy to be bolder in everything you do — what you ask for, what action you take and what goals you have.

I remember attending Richard Branson's launch event for his book *Finding My Virginity* back in October 2017 at the Troxy, London. He was being interviewed on stage in front of an audience of around 2,000 people about his entrepreneurial journey to date. It was during one of the intervals that

I witnessed a member of the audience act with audacity. As the crowd was being entertained by a musical performance on the other side of the stage to where Branson and the host sat, this person folded up a sheet of paper into an aeroplane and threw it in Branson's direction. As the band finished, Branson picked up this piece of paper that had landed on his lap and realized that a member of the audience had just pitched their business to him in a rather creative way.

It was memorable.

More importantly, it got his attention.

I don't know what came of this afterwards, but given how he wrote about it in his blog a few days after, I'm pretty sure that he at least read through what was inside that paper aeroplane. For me, it was a beautiful demonstration of the fact that if you don't try, you'll never know, and if you don't ask, the answer will always be no.

If we want to achieve more and live a better story, we must constantly remind ourselves of what matters most and commit to building our lives around those things. We get what we commit to. What are you telling the world that you are committed to through the actions you are currently taking?

Focus on consistency over intensity

During his acceptance speech after winning the Outstanding Actor in a Motion Picture Award for his role in the film *Fences*, Denzel Washington told the audience at the National Association for the Advancement of Colored People (NAACP) Image Awards that, 'Without commitment, you will never start. But more importantly, without consistency, you will never finish.'

Mike Tyson also highlighted the importance of consistency when reflecting back on his boxing career. Repeating a daily routine over a number of years allowed him to take advantage of the compound effect – evenings would be spent studying the best boxers at the time by watching videos of their fights and early mornings would be spent running three to five miles, followed by training in the gym and ring. The result? In November 1986, the twenty-year-old Tyson knocked out thirty-three-year-old Trevor Berbick in under six minutes, to become the youngest heavyweight champion in the history of boxing.

The recognition that Washington received and the records that Tyson broke were not overnight journeys. They rarely are. Success in any endeavour is a slow, gradual process that ultimately rewards those who can consistently follow the path and do the work that the majority are simply not willing to do.

It isn't particularly sexy or glamorous.

Dig deeper into nearly every 'overnight success story' and you will discover years of hard work, sacrifices and persistence. And it's this ability to live each day with intention that will be one of the most valuable traits you can develop, because extraordinary achievement is always preceded by extraordinary consistency. Falling in love with starting is very easy; falling in love with the work itself, the process and the journey, however, is hard.

Success isn't a random act, and people don't rise from nothing.

Too many of us pray for colossal changes and results today, but fail to appreciate that if what you desire is really important, you will enjoy the climb as much as the view at the summit. Successful outcomes are rarely the result of a single choice but are built up through good choices over time.

Powerful micro-choices informed by a strategic macro-perspective leads to extraordinary results.

The question is whether the dream means so much to you that you are willing to go after it for as long as it takes?

To become a success story, you must be willing to look stupid and like a beginner for a long time before you start getting things right. Consistency grows out of your ability to be patient with the process of taking small steps forward each day. Too many of us, however, give up far too early because we aren't making progress fast enough. Our impatience becomes an energetic block to our progress.

What is the alternative?

The time will pass anyway, so why not make it your ally and keep going, comfortable in the knowledge that we all travel at different speeds. Many of our deepest desires might feel impossible feats in the short term, but what about the long term? You will suck at most things in the beginning; the truth is that your first of anything will probably be awful but you can't make your twenty-fifth, twenty-sixth and twenty-seventh of anything without making your first. It takes commitment, consistency and patience to create your most amazing work. Use the months and years ahead to arrive at a place that will make you proud, because each day that you keep moving forward is another day where billions around the world will give up and go home.

We must have patience in the journey and a disciplined focus on consistency around the daily habits and routines that will inch us closer towards our dreams.

The goal isn't to be better than anyone else, it's simply to be better than who you were yesterday. Slow progress is always better than no progress, so eliminate the idea of perfection and instead see yourself as a never-ending work in progress.

Once you do, it will liberate you. As Lao Tzu said, 'Nature does not hurry, yet everything is accomplished.' And that feeling of progress and momentum? It's one of the most energizing feelings of all.

None of us know for sure what lies ahead and whether we will succeed, but the moment we decide to act, the next step towards realizing our vision is revealed. And that next step is all you need to see in order to take action. You don't get to see the entire map at the start, it appears as you set off into the magic of the unknown. As an entrepreneur friend of mine once said to me, 'When everything is unknown, brother, anything is possible.' If you want greater clarity, you must keep moving forward. Sometimes it can take ten years to get that one year that will completely change your life. Forever.

Take a moment right now to reflect on the following . . .

1. If you took your average day right now and repeated it every day for the next five years, do you feel that you would be closer to where you would like to be or further away?
2. What does this tell you about your habits?
3. If you feel that your current daily habits are holding you back, what must change and when will it?

Consistency can be hard, especially when you are at the beginning. What makes it easier, however, is your ability to enjoy the process of pursuit – the more fun, exciting and interesting it is, the more likely you are to stick with it.

A client of mine, for example, didn't particularly enjoy the feeling of getting rejected when approaching new prospects. James had recently set up his own consulting business and was finding it tough to win clients. With each rejection, he collapsed into a deep hole of overthinking about what went wrong, and these unproductive thoughts negatively affected how he showed up for the next meeting. It was a cycle that he had to step away from.

The first thing that we did was to help change his reflective process: after each meeting – regardless of the outcome – I got him to send me his thoughts on what went well and what could be improved for next time. We channelled his energy towards more productive thinking – learning from each new interaction and coming back stronger for the next.

The second thing I did was to help gamify the process by turning his negative experience with rejection into something positive.

We all love taking on a challenge, so I set him one: his mission, should he choose to accept it, was to get rejected 100 times in ninety days.

In this way, he didn't have the time to dwell on the last rejection as he thought about where he was going to get his next one from. I remember having a call with him close to the end of this time frame, when he told me that he wasn't going to be able to get anywhere close to 100.

He then paused, before his excitement spilled over.

The reason was because he had just landed his twelfth yes. And this was exactly the objective of the challenge. It's why the best salespeople focus more on the number of people they're contacting each day over the number of contracts that are being signed. You must give yourself opportunities to try, to learn and to succeed. And the more conversations he had, the closer he was to that first yes. When you have a game to play, as James did, your energy isn't a problem. With no game, no plan and no direction, however, your energy suffers. How can you bring this concept of gamification into your life to make the journey more fun and exciting?

Life is an infinite process of becoming more than who we were yesterday, so it's important for you to not let temporary breaks along the way turn into permanent exiles from the path ahead. Make decisions today with a long-term perspective in mind, because when you consistently show up and put in the work necessary, you will discover the energy to become as successful as you choose to be.

REWIRE

Upgrade your mental game. Silence the inner critic so that you may listen to the guide within. Speak to yourself in the same way you would to someone you care about. Be your own placebo. Become the hero of your story. Fight for what matters. Turn obstacles into opportunities. Remind yourself of just how far you have come. Focus your energy on that which you can control. Adapt to survive, innovate and thrive. Learn from your failures; see them as stepping stones to success. Small, consistent steps lead to big things over time. Begin before you're ready. Focus on progress over perfection and consistency over intensity.

+

PART 3

Protect Your Personal Energy

7
Manage Your Energy, Not Your Time

'When you channel your energy correctly you actually generate energy; when you do not, you divert energy into frustration, procrastination, exasperation and many other "ations".'

COLIN TURNER

In our everyday lives, our attention and energy can so easily be stolen by the distractions of social media, TV, shiny object syndrome and consumerism. This fear of missing out – on that new TV series that everyone is talking about, the new social media app that everyone is joining, or those notifications that are always popping up and keeping us chained to our devices – is what can keep us from spending time on what we say our priorities are and alone with our thoughts, exploring the infinite depths, wonders and universe of our imagination.

This is not to say that these distractions are inherently bad – after all, they are merely resources and tools. However, we must be conscious about how we use them and the role that they play in our lives. If we're not careful, they will kill our energy, momentum and creativity.

This is where the role of energy management comes in.

If we are to radically transform the way we live and work, it begins with our ability to manage our energy effectively. Just like we have speed limits on roads to protect drivers from vehicle accidents, we must also embrace the same for life, to protect our energy and thrive over the long term. You can't live life at 150 m.p.h. and expect to be immune from burning out and facing frequent energy crashes.

In the first two parts of this book, we explored how to awaken your power and rewire your energetic state. In this third part, we will look at how to protect your personal energy by managing it better, understanding the impact that your environment can have and developing a better relationship with money. Without boundaries to protect your energy, you will never experience true freedom and fulfilment because you simply won't have any energy left to do the things that you want to do.

When Charlie Rose interviewed billionaires Warren Buffett and Bill Gates, he asked Gates what he had learnt from being friends with Buffett for nearly three decades. The first lesson he shared was that it's not necessarily a good idea to leave large sums of money to your children. It made him think about how he was going to give his wealth away and acted as a catalyst for him directing it towards philanthropic causes.

The second lesson came after looking through Buffett's calendar. He noticed that there were often days where nothing at all was scheduled. His calendar, however, had always been full. Full of meetings, things to do and projects to work on. Gates learnt that an overscheduled calendar was no way to live and saw the importance of embracing white space in our daily and weekly schedules, if we are to make the most of our energy. You can do amazing things, but only if you have the energy to do them.

When you rush life, you fail to appreciate this greatest of gifts. When you live slower, however, you begin to savour all the beauty that surrounds us – from the microscopic to the macroscopic – and possess the energy to focus on the people and things that matter most. Taking regular breaks in your day doesn't make you less productive. In fact, the opposite is more likely to happen. By taking lunchtime breaks to detach from work, for example, you feel less exhausted and more energized upon returning to your desk. With a clearer mind and sharper focus, you become more productive during those afternoon hours.

We also get our best insights when the mind is still, because connection to our wisdom that lies within can only be made when we schedule regular time for reflection and thinking. 'When the brain relaxes, it's like a sedimentation process in action,' says marketing strategist and cartoonist Sean D'Souza. 'The millions of thoughts you have sink to the bottom and the most path-breaking thoughts float to the top like cream.' In an overstimulated world, being mindful is a superpower. By scheduling regular time to rest and recharge, you begin to unlock your greatest source of creativity:

- Isaac Newton discovered gravity while sitting under a tree and being hit on the head by a falling apple.
- Ruth Handler was inspired to create the Barbie doll during a holiday trip that her family took to Switzerland.
- Thomas Edison got fresh insights by spending an hour almost every day sitting at the end of a dock

and fishing. He never did catch any fish, but that was never his intention. With no bait used, no one would disturb him, not even the fish.

- J. K. Rowling's idea for the Harry Potter series of books came to her while stuck on a train from Manchester to London. The delay gave her mind the opportunity to wander, and by the time she arrived in London, she was energized by a vision already being mapped out in her head.
- Albert Einstein got the inspiration he needed when grappling with complex problems by turning to classical music.

We mistakenly think that significant breakthroughs occur after long hours in the library or office, but that's not where the magic of fresh insight lives. Your best ideas nearly always come away from the desk and screens. In order to live better and achieve more, therefore, you must carve out protected space within your calendar to recharge and to nurture your creativity.

Become your own Chief Energy Officer

When you're working towards an extraordinary vision, you must make effective use of the periods in your day where your energy is at its highest. Your level of energy first thing in the morning, for example, will be different to your level after lunch and in the early evening. And it is your knowledge of this that can help dictate how you make better use of your time.

Just think how many of us put off that visit to the gym or that task we know needs doing until later in the day, in the

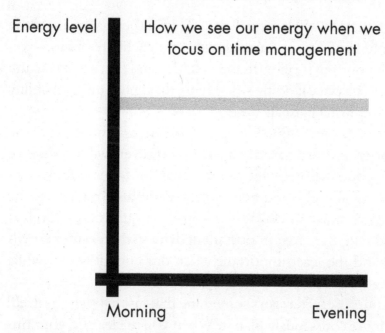

Energy level

How we see our energy when we
focus on time management

Morning   Evening

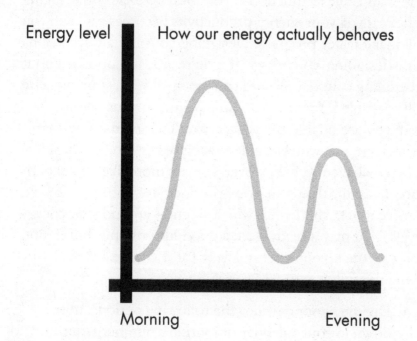

Energy level

How our energy actually behaves

Morning   Evening

belief that we will be equally as effective then as we are at the beginning of the day. You already know what happens – you end up putting it off until the next day and that's because the longer you put off doing something, the higher the probability that you won't actually do it.

Some people enjoy high levels of energy throughout the majority of their day. Most of us, however, will experience energy fluctuations, which means that our focus and productivity will also ebb and flow in sync with this. To increase the latter, we must therefore work around our energy levels – scheduling the most important activities when our energy is high and the least important when our energy is low, while taking frequent breaks to rest with intention.

A purposeful day isn't something that just happens by itself; you must consciously plan it. When you're clear on your priorities and able to function at your best because you're taking better care of your energy, productivity becomes easy and you will make faster progress. Designing your life always begins with designing your days. If you're not intentional about scheduling your day around your energy levels, someone else will schedule it for you with little regard to your energy.

If you are unable to manage your energy in a way that is sustainable, you won't be able to achieve anything of meaning. When managed well, however, you are more likely to experience quantum leaps in your productivity and, as a result, achieve more. This begins with awareness around your energy levels. You may already have a good idea of this, but if not, you can track your energy levels for a couple of weeks by doing the following:

1. Dividing your day into the following periods, note down in your calendar or journal a number from

1 to 10 (10 being the highest) that best sums up your energy level: early morning (waking up until breakfast), late morning (after breakfast until lunch), early afternoon, late afternoon, evening (after dinner).

2. Next to each number, note down your observations about what is giving you energy or draining you of energy. Beginning my day with exercise, visualization and journalling, for example, contributes to my high energy levels during the morning periods. I'm also able to notice just how much my energy is negatively impacted on days when I'm unable to exercise or leave the house.

3. Do this for at least two weeks, to get a feel for your energy and an understanding of what times of day you tend to experience higher and lower levels of energy. Notice whether there are any observable patterns.

4. Reflect also on whether there are days where you feel more energized and less energized. As an example, Monday tends to be the day that my corporate clients have identified as their lowest energy day, while my self-employed clients see it as their highest energy day.

5. Repeat the above in the middle of each quarter, as seasonal changes can have an impact on your energy levels.

Conducting some simple observations like this will give you a better understanding of your physical and mental energy, as well as an insight into how your energy levels are affected by your habits, environment and other factors. This information makes you a better Chief Energy Officer of your life by helping you structure your day, week and month around your expected energy levels. An hour of doing deep work when your energy is high will be as effective as attempting the same task over four hours when your energy is low. In fact, if you attempt to get your most important work done when you lack energy, the quality of what you produce will suffer heavily and you will be very easily distracted.

Here are some other thoughts to keep in mind so that you can maximize your periods of high and low energy:

A. High energy periods

1. These will be your most productive periods and as a result must be protected for activities that demand more energy, such as writing, preparing for a presentation or project planning. The earlier that you get your most important work done when your energy is high, the more productive you will feel, regardless of what else you get done later in the day. And if you're unsure as to what to spend this energy on, ask yourself this question when weighing up your options: 'Given who and where I want to be, is this the best use of my energy?'

2. Remove unnecessary energy drains during these periods so that you can be completely present and fully immersed in whatever you're doing. Switch your phone to flight mode, block these periods out in your calendar so that focus and energy can't be stolen from you by a last-minute meeting taking its place, and make sure the physical environment around you is well organized.

3. An understanding of when these periods occur can help you make smarter choices. If mornings are when your energy is high, you can turn your commute to productive instead of dead time by listening to audiobooks, brainstorming ideas for a project or getting some writing done by using an app that converts your voice dictation into words that you can later review.

B. Low energy periods

1. Use these periods at the end of the day to plan and prepare for the next. It will not only save you energy and time the following morning when you know what your priorities are, but also help you sleep better now that your thoughts have been transferred to paper.
2. Routine activities such as administrative tasks and checking of emails and social media should be reserved for these moments. The trap that many of us fall into is that we do these first thing in the day and therefore sacrifice energy that could have been better spent elsewhere.
3. As you get familiar with when these periods occur, you can use them as opportunities to completely disconnect. I reserve at least one day a week and one week a quarter for this as an example.

When you're energized, it's so much easier to make smarter choices about how you spend your time. And by also listening to what your energy is telling you and developing a better relationship with it, you give yourself the freedom to respond accordingly and experience greater clarity of mind. The quantum leaps in your productivity will translate into you achieving more and, as a result, equip you with energy to dive deeper into all that can be possible.

Establish energetic shields to protect your energy

When you're travelling by air, flight attendants gather at the front before take-off to demonstrate the aeroplane's safety procedures in case of an emergency.

During these demonstrations, they instruct you to put on your oxygen mask first before helping others to do so. It's something that we can and must also apply to our own lives in order to protect our energy – if you don't take care of yourself first, you won't be able to help others, and if you don't establish energetic shields around you, you'll never be in control of your energy. Help others without first putting on your oxygen mask and you will eventually run out of air. Put yours on first, however, and you can go on to help significantly more people.

How often do you find yourself doing something just to make someone else happy at the cost of your own personal energy?

In order for us to make effective use of the periods in our day when our energy level is at its highest, we must establish energetic shields so that we are not taken advantage of. If you don't, these shields will be set for you by others and you will very quickly become disconnected from who you truly are. You will end up wasting precious time on things that add little value to your life.

Setting up energetic shields isn't selfish, it is self-care at its deepest level through the act of self-love.

In the words of Rachel Wolchin, 'Givers need to set limits because takers rarely do.' Enjoying a more fulfilling life is as much about the process of eliminating the toxic behaviours and activities that are holding you back as it is about the addition of healthier habits and decisions. Once you stop prioritizing other people's needs over your own, you find yourself in a position to address those things that will help you make real progress in what matters most.

While some of us find it easy to say no, most of us can find this a struggle – we worry about what others will think of us, whether they will believe our excuses, or the potential conflict that may arise. Most of us live our lives trying to please others. Instead of living as our true selves, we tend to live out of our ego; that ego which needs to be chosen, validated and liked. Unfortunately, if we are consumed with worry about how we will be judged by others, we will never achieve anything worthwhile.

It's important to understand that if those around you consider themselves to be real friends, they will respect the energetic shields you feel you need to have in order to function at your best. Those who get upset are very likely the ones who have benefited the most from the absence of any energetic shields set by you. If you want to avoid receiving a fast-track ticket to burnout and exhaustion, you must understand that you don't need to say yes to everything.

Here's something to reflect on that illustrates the importance of having energetic shields set up to protect your energy: 'If I'm saying yes to this, what am I saying no to?'

We can easily overlook the fact that by saying yes to something that doesn't align with our values, we are saying no to more free time, to activities that we actually want to do or to the very thing that can help take us to that next level of our lives. Saying yes to others can often mean saying no to yourself, so make sure you reflect on this question before making your choices: 'Does saying yes to this bring me closer to or further away from the sort of life I want to live?' Because when you say yes to things you really mean no to, you are giving your energy away to things that will drain you.

During an interview that I did with Bob Burg, co-author of the *Go-Giver* series of books and an incredible mentor of mine, we explored the importance of being able to say no to requests and invitations that you really don't want to accept. One of the questions that I was curious to get his thoughts on was how to handle this with grace and kindness, such that we can protect our energy for what matters most without feeling guilty.

'Firstly, please don't ever confuse being nice with not taking care of yourself and your personal needs,' said Burg. 'Now let's use the very generic situation where someone asks you to do something that you don't want to do, like serving on a committee. When this occurs, offer lavish appreciation just for their thinking of you, decline and then end with more gratitude.' Knowing how to say no respectfully to anything that you don't feel an absolute hell yes for will help support and protect your energy.

Burg continued by sharing an example of how this could be applied: 'I would look to say something like, "Thank you for your kind offer. While it's not something I choose to pursue, please know how honoured I am to have been asked." They may persist of course, but all you need to do here is to reply with, "I'd just rather not, but thank you so much for considering me." This is key. Do not make an excuse for saying no. If you start saying things like "I don't have the time at this moment" or "I don't feel I'm qualified to make a success of this", then they will attempt to answer your objections and continue to persuade you. And should they overcome your objections, you will eventually be cornered into accepting.'

Establishing energetic shields around you helps to protect your energy by preventing things from spiralling out of control, and is why deciding what not to do is as important as deciding what to do. Saying no to that late-night party can be the difference between waking up the next morning feeling fully recharged for work and feeling hung-over and exhausted. Saying no to meaningless work is what creates the space for living with passion and purpose. Saying no to busyness gives you the energy to live life and experience all the beauty, wonder and adventure that it has to offer. All of this contributes to you enjoying life more, and as a result you end up having the energy to share more of who you truly are with the world.

Write your not-to-do list

You have heard of to-do lists and may even use these in your daily life. But have you ever put together a not-to-do list – a list of things that you don't do no matter what?

If habits are the non-negotiable activities that you do daily to elevate and recharge your energy, then the items on a not-to-do list are the non-negotiable activities that you don't do daily. You simply say no to them or you outsource them. Doing so will stop you giving your energy away to the things you don't want in your life and automatically channel that energy instead into the things you want to do.

When I first compiled my own not-to-do list, one of the items that helped to protect my energy and continue moving forward in my personal growth journey was 'No to dealing with and responding to haters'. Don't get me wrong, I welcome valid criticism, especially from those whose work I admire, because it helps me improve. However, there's a big difference between receiving thoughtful criticism that can make you better at what you do and a troll who is simply trying to get an emotional reaction from you. I remember when I first started sharing videos on YouTube I got a comment from a user saying, 'Go get a real job and learn how to speak English properly.' I was tempted to respond, but quickly remembered that this was a non-negotiable activity that I had consciously chosen not to participate in. And with nearly eight billion people on this planet of ours, I didn't want to be discouraged by the words of one.

It also taught me a lesson about having the courage to show up every day as your true self: haters come with the territory; it's part of the game. Don't take it personally, because you will simply be wasting your energy. In fact, it's important to keep in mind that you will rarely – if ever – be hated by someone who is doing more than you, because their energy is focused on their own journey. Use that energy instead towards turning that vision for your life into reality, and in this process of realizing your potential there will be people inspired by your journey, following you for the courage you demonstrate and grateful for the value you bring into their lives.

Here's how you can start preparing your own not-to-do list:

1. Open your calendar or diary and look at the last full calendar month so that you can see how your time was spent.

2. Review the activities you did, especially the recurring ones, and label each as 'high-value' or 'low-value'.

3. For the low-value activities, reflect on how you feel about them and which of these you can stop doing or outsource in order to create space for the more high-value activities.

4. Use this to help put your not-to-do list together. Keep it to a maximum of ten items, so that they are easy to remember and don't overwhelm you.

Time and energy are limited resources, and how you choose to spend these matters. As management consultant and author Allison Rimm wrote in a *Harvard Business Review* article, 'Once you accept that you have more to do than time to do it all, that is actually a liberating concept. This realization forces you to acknowledge there are lower priority items that you will likely never complete. Delete those non-essentials, put them on your not-to-do list, and commit to letting them go. This will prevent you from wasting precious time continually re-evaluating whether you might get to them that could be better invested in actually completing your work.' In fact, one of the fastest ways to progress in life is less about doing more and more about saying no to the activities that are currently holding you back. We get caught up in everything that we feel we should do and forget what we must stop doing.

When a client of mine used her not-to-do list to establish energetic shields around her, the results were nothing short of transformational in every way. Her quality of life improved so dramatically that she is often asked to share her story with others, and the results that she delivered at work started to get people's attention.

She is a fund manager who oversees billions of dollars in assets that are invested in the shares of companies she believes will deliver a handsome return to both her and her clients across market cycles. However, when she gave birth to her first child, she was concerned that on returning to work it would be difficult to maintain a healthy balance between her domestic and professional lives while working towards her career goals. During one of our coaching sessions, we agreed to placing an energetic shield between work and home with the item, 'No work after 4.30 p.m.'

Following the implementation of this, alongside other items on her not-to-do list, the performance of her fund began to significantly out-perform the market and peer groups. When I asked her what she felt contributed to this, she said, 'Knowing that I have to switch off from work by the time the clock strikes 4.30 p.m. and that I can't take that work home makes me more productive and decisive. I used to take hours trying to make an investment decision – questioning my thoughts and my team's analysis of the opportunity. I don't have that luxury now. If I want to come home and spend the evening and weekends with my family without being chained to work, I had to be more decisive. I had to listen to my intuition more. And, so far, it seems to be working.'

Slow down in order to speed up

In the second-floor atrium of the Museum of Modern Art (MoMA) in New York, the small plaque detailed a simple instruction to visitors: 'Sit silently with the artist for a duration of your choosing.' Behind it stood a queue of visitors eager to enter a large square space and sit down – one at a time – at a wooden table opposite the artist Marina Abramović, whose hair in a braided plait was pulled forward over her left shoulder.

This would be one of the longest pieces of performance art on record, and certainly the one with the largest audience.

The artist would be sitting with her hands in her lap, six days a week, seven hours a day, for two and a half months, in a chair under bright lights, inviting the public to engage in silent conversation in front of a live audience. No food. No water. No breaks. To prepare, the artist had trained with Tibetan Buddhists and noted how she was able to transcend the limits of her own body and mind through meditation. She trained like NASA trains astronauts – getting both her body and mind in the best possible shape through rigorous preparation.

By the time the performance ended, close to 1,400 people had sat opposite the artist. Men and women, young and old, cried, smiled, sat and stared as they basked in the shared spotlight. Some sat for just a few minutes, some for hours and others for an entire day. It was a very public affair and at the same time intensely private. Each engagement delivered a non-verbal exchange of curiosity, feeling and understanding as it danced in the realms of the psychological and spiritual. Emotional energy was exchanged through the sound of silence.

A young girl who sat across from the artist stood up after seventy-five minutes, declaring that she had lost all sense of time and thought that she had only been with the artist for just a few minutes.

An older man, with wrinkles etched across his forehead under the shade of his messy grey hair, sat down for around twenty minutes. The two of them gazed deep into the universe of each other's eyes. The artist didn't smile and hardly blinked. She was completely still throughout. The man, meanwhile, shuffled his feet and twitched his hands, as his head and eyes remained utterly focused. Upon finally leaving the chair, he made his way to the back of the towering atrium and leant his forehead against the wall.

A young man with shoulder-length curls took to the chair, with the artist maintaining the same gaze she had given everyone before him – a gentle yet intent gaze. Silence descended throughout the atrium as it became clear that this young man was weeping. As his eyes continued to gaze, tears were swimming down the contours of his face. After some time, the artist also began to weep in the same silent passive way. Everyone waiting in line and watching what was unfolding became hooked. Many were also overcome with tears.

In an age of increasing demands on our attention and the busyness of everyday life, sitting still in a space of silence isn't a quality that many of us would feel we are particularly good at.

However, in this performance entitled *The Artist Is Present*, the idea of actually connecting with somebody and being asked to do something as simple as sit and look at the face of a complete stranger somehow really spoke to people. I've read that couples who have been together for decades can sit in silence and understand one another perfectly. I've done this with my wife and the experience proved to be as intimate, emotional and bonding as I had imagined. There were tears, there were hugs and we felt that the appreciation we had for each other had significantly deepened.

Who would've thought that this sort of intimacy could also exist between two total strangers?

Abramović's performance showed that it could. And in the

process, she created a space of silence that many who sat in that chair will never forget. In the energy of stillness, an entire parallel universe opened up that would otherwise be invisible because of how much we are always in motion, and it was within this other world that people felt things they could never imagine feeling normally.

When interviewed, she shared that, 'The idea of this piece was to be in the present – absolutely in the moment. Not in the past which has happened. Not in the future that hasn't happened, but just in that moment. Your mind doesn't go anywhere else. You are in the here and now – and not only the here and now in myself, but also in the person sitting opposite you.' And when asked about the strangers that sat across from her, she added that, 'They would enter this zone where sound disappears, I disappear. They become the mirrors of themselves. And these incredible emotions surfaced – I heard so many people crying.'

What does it mean to be here now, to live in the present moment?

I believe it means to channel your energy, senses and awareness to what is happening right now in front of you, free of judgement. Most of us struggle to be present in our daily lives, but this present moment is all you have and is where your future is manufactured. Nothing exists except this current moment, and it's the only time that you can have a direct influence on. It reconnects you to the energy that is flowing inside of us, waiting to be channelled in ways that will soothe your spirit and soul.

In the documentary *The Last Dance*, which chronicled Michael Jordan's career with the Chicago Bulls, biographer Mark Vancil was asked what made Jordan such a great player. He responded by saying: 'Most people struggle to be present.

People go and sit in ashrams for twenty years in India trying to be present. Michael's a mystic. He was never anywhere else. His gift was not that he could jump high, run fast, shoot a basketball. His gift was that he was completely present. And that was the separator.'

The past has already happened, and while we can learn from it and redefine our interpretation of an event, we must be careful not to slip into the unhealthy habit of spending too much time dwelling on it and worrying about it. Learn to let go, learn to accept and learn to forgive – whether that's forgiving yourself or others. As Amit Ray noted so beautifully, 'If you want to fly in the sky you need to leave the earth. If you want to move forward, you need to let go of the past that drags you down.' Once we have released the baggage of our past, our focus on what is most important sharpens and we discover the energy to move on to a better tomorrow.

And the future?

While it can inspire us and help us plan today for it, we must not get so caught up in anticipation of what comes next that we forget the present, we forget to live. If you're always living for the future, you will be trapped in a chamber of anxiety. When you have greater awareness in the moment, you will discover joy and happiness in the simplest of things. Wisdom has also taught me not to worry about trying to predict what will happen next week, next month or next year. Instead, I have learnt to focus on the now, on what I can control today.

Take a moment to practise this simple breathing exercise to feel what it's like to ground yourself back in the present. Follow this with your eyes open, get someone to read it out to you so that you may close your eyes, or record yourself reading it so that you may play it back whenever you need to.

1. Place the palm of one of your hands across the front of your stomach and the other across the middle of your chest.

2. Take a few moments now to connect with the rhythmic movement of your breathing. You want to be breathing in slowly through the nose with your stomach expanding, then out through the mouth with your stomach contracting back in.

3. Now gently bring your energy down towards your feet, out to each of the toes and notice the sensations you feel. From this place of connection, follow your breath all the way down to your feet as you inhale, then back out again as your breath bounces back up from the base of your feet. Do this for a couple of breaths.

4. Bring your energy up now in turn to your legs, stomach, chest, hands, arms, back, shoulders and head. As you connect with each body part, notice the sensations you feel and follow your breath down and up from this place for a couple of breaths.

5. Notice how any tension there is within you begins to melt away as you continue with this rhythmic breathing, and how you now feel lighter, calmer and more relaxed.

6. It's completely normal if your mind begins to wander, with thoughts rising and falling from within. Think of these thoughts as soft clouds floating through your mind, noticing the nature of them with curiosity but not attaching yourself to any of them. And then gently bring your energy back to the present moment and your breathing.

7. From this place of calm, bring your energy now to the sensations you are feeling across your entire body. Imagine a bright light spreading out from under the two palms of your hands that are placed across your chest and stomach. See this energetic light expand and spread out across where you are in this moment, the street you live on, the country you reside in and the planet we all share. Notice how connected your energy is to everything that surrounds you.

8. Wriggle your toes and fingers as you gently bring your energy back to your breath and where you are in this moment. Listen closely to the sounds around you, and as you slowly open your eyes, notice how you begin to move forward in your day with greater purpose, precision and presence.

During those moments where you feel anxious, afraid or worried about the past or future, you can ground yourself back into the present moment by concentrating your energy on your breath. Most of us aren't aware about just how much the way we breathe influences our energy; put simply, more oxygen equals more energy. It's like giving your mind a long, hot bath – you come out of this mindful practice feeling rejuvenated, relaxed and ready to take on whatever challenges await.

'Touching the present moment does not mean getting rid of the past or the future. As you touch the present moment, you realize that the present is made of the past and is creating the future. Touching the present, you touch the past and the future at the same time. You touch globally the infinity of time, the ultimate dimension of reality,' wrote Thich Nhat

Hanh. In this age of busyness and distraction, nothing is as beautiful as living in the now and having a deeper connection to what you are experiencing moment-to-moment in the present.

This energy of stillness can be truly transformative in nature, as San Francisco-based Visitacion Valley middle school discovered. Surrounded by drugs and gang violence, students were stressed out and agitated. There would be frequent fighting in the corridors, graffiti scrawled over the walls and cursing aimed directly at teachers. Absenteeism rates were among the city's highest and so were suspensions, and exhausted teachers routinely called in sick.

One morning, the teachers arrived at school to find three dead bodies dumped in the schoolyard. One of them shared how there had been thirty-eight killings within the school's neighbourhood in 2006 and how students were impacted by violence within the community. Murders were so frequent that the school employed a full-time grief counsellor to support those most affected.

In 2007, a meditation programme called Quiet Time was brought in to address some of these challenges. Teachers were understandably sceptical at first, given how often they were asked to implement new ideas with their students and the fact that they would be the first public school nationwide to adopt this programme. However, just a month after it started, there were already reports that students appeared happier.

They were working harder, growing more attentive in class, easier to teach, and the number of fights fell dramatically. Introduced to all age groups, the programme saw students sit for fifteen minutes of meditation twice a day. Classes took place at their desks after a bell was rung, and during this period of stillness they repeated a personal mantra in their heads until they entered a deep state of relaxation. And sometimes the entire school met to meditate together in assemblies.

Within just a year, student suspensions fell by 45%, and within a couple of years, attendance rates were over 98% (some of the highest in the city).

By 2015, 20% of graduates were admitted to the highly academic Lowell high school. Prior to this, it was rare for even one student from Visitacion Valley to be accepted. Furthermore, the state's education department found their students to be the happiest in the whole of San Francisco.

The calming influence of the meditation programme literally transformed their future. It helped them to navigate the everyday stresses that they were exposed to in their lives. The results that were achieved at Visitacion Valley led to more schools across the city introducing a similar programme. While there is still violence within the community, the students have become less affected by it. They're more comfortable with sharing their feelings, seeking peace from within and moving on.

When was the last time you completely disconnected from work and your phone – checking email, scrolling through social media feeds and sitting through back-to-back meetings – for any extended period of time?

Meditation is like exercise for the mind – it brings us closer to our ideal self, pulls us back from the chaos of our daily lives and helps us to get better at life. As this Zen saying wisely highlights: 'We cannot see our reflection in running water. It is only in still water that we can see.' It's in this energy of stillness that we appreciate that silence isn't empty; it's full of answers. It gives our innate wisdom a voice, allows our creativity to blossom and brings clarity to our minds.

There's a very good reason why we hear this meditation

advice again and again, especially from some of the most successful people on the planet. The activity helps us to settle emotionally, and, according to the Greater Good Science Center at the University of California, Berkeley, it sharpens our attention, increases our resilience to stress and our capacity for compassion, can have a positive impact on our relationships and can even improve our physical health. When you recharge yourself through the energy of presence, you gain greater control over your emotional energy and your response to events outside of your control.

Step back from the waterfall

Think of your mind like a waterfall – this endless stream of thoughts crashing down and flooding your mind with anxiety. It will drain your energy if you're not careful and wash you away towards a rollercoaster of overwhelm. If you're always stuck standing beneath it, it can be loud and intimidating.

If you step back and stand in that space behind the waterfall, however, you separate yourself from the noise and are able to observe each droplet of thought without being weighed down by it.

This is the first step you must take if you want to access that well of creative wisdom that is buried within us. We all have it. But until you prioritize time to step away from that waterfall, you will forever be trapped in a never-ending cycle of busyness. In the chaos of our busy lives, never underestimate the value of stillness, because it's here that we can build a deeper connection with that voice from within. That inner wisdom, guide and true self.

When my computer freezes or crashes, my immediate action

is to turn the device off, unplug it and then plug it back in again. That same process applies to you – simply unplugging ourselves to recharge can be the very thing that is required to reboot our own inner computer. Even a short break away from the busyness of work can send you back with more energy, focus and creativity.

While it's important for you to be as intentional with your rest periods as with your work, the unfortunate reality is that many of us don't know how to properly recharge. Instead, we sabotage the time we have away from work by diving deeper into distractions such as our smartphones and as a result drain more of our energy.

By slowing down and honouring these times of intentional rest, you give yourself the opportunity to recharge, regenerate and rejuvenate. Energy must be recharged, or it runs out and you lose the ability to maximize the full extent of your capabilities.

Take time for purposeful breaks.

Take time to connect with nature.

Take time for yourself to do nothing.

Take time to explore your hobbies.

Take time to stare up at the sky.

Take time to be with people you care about.

Take time to get lost in a fiction book.

Take time to discover new places.

It's in this space of slowing down that our brain is able to process everything that it has absorbed and transform this randomness of thought into creative breakthroughs. More often than not, it's where our best ideas originate from, where insight is born and where the clarity to make better decisions is found. 'If everyone visited their local parks for half an hour each week there would be 7% fewer cases of depression and

9% fewer cases of high blood pressure,' notes Australian researcher Dr Danielle Shanahan.

Ask any world-class athlete about the factors that have helped them succeed, and it's very likely that they will talk as much about getting sufficient rest in the days and weeks before a major event as they will about their training regime. They understand that recovery and renewal are essential in order to perform and function at our best. It's also important to keep in mind that the quality of our rest periods influences the quality of our productivity time.

Given the above, I was therefore not surprised when I learnt how organizations are increasingly making employee wellbeing a key priority. It makes sense when you think about it: a well-rested employee leads to a more productive employee and a more productive employee leads to a more profitable business. In contrast, an employee who is regularly over-worked will sooner or later experience a significant drop in their productivity and personal energy, and an unhealthy spike in their feelings of exhaustion and stress.

Whatever your idea of working hard and being productive looks like, it must include the energetically recharging activities of slowing down and introspective reflection. If you are constantly in doing mode, you are sacrificing the opportunity to have your own 'Eureka!' moments and savour the beauty of life.

8
Electrify Your Environment

*'Environment is the invisible hand that
shapes human behaviour.'*

JAMES CLEAR

Your environment has a far bigger impact on your success and wellbeing than you can imagine. And for this simple reason: you can't swim in a river of negative energy and expect a positive result. Your level of talent and potential is completely meaningless if you are surrounded by those who won't or can't help you unleash it.

We are like sponges in the sense that we soak up the energies that we are surrounded with. The energy of people, places and things rubs off on you, whether you like it or not. It influences your behaviour through how you think, what you believe in and how you act, and this will either anchor you down or energize you forward.

Because the quality of your life is determined by the quality of your input, you must make sure that you are regularly reviewing, optimizing and electrifying your environment such that it aligns with the person that you want to be. You've got to ask yourself how much time you are spending around people who deplete you of energy, and change things if it's an answer that is costing you progress towards your vision.

Since I began taking better care of my energy and full responsibility for my life, I have been keen to surround myself with energizers who could challenge me to level up, raise my standards and become a better human. It led to me building a friendship with Marc Alfred Tidd, who quickly became my first business mentor. Here was a guy that lived and breathed entrepreneurship – someone who could guide me along the path from where I was to where I wanted to be. Our energies must've vibrated at a similar frequency, because by the end of our first meeting, at a mutual friend's birthday party, he extended an invitation for me to join a mastermind group that he was facilitating. I first came across this concept when reading Napoleon Hill's book *Think and Grow Rich*. Hill shared that the objective of such a group was to help members achieve their goals through mutual support, learning from a diverse set of perspectives and accountability. I accepted Tidd's invitation, and while I had no idea of what to expect, the experience would come to energize my mind in ways I could never have predicted.

The first group meeting was to be held inside the Ritz in London – one of the world's most iconic hotels. I was excited; not just about the other members that I would be meeting but because it would be my first time inside this glamorous hotel. So much so that I finished up at work early in order to arrive on time.

I was one of fifteen members that made up the group, and

after we all arrived, Tidd got us to introduce ourselves to each other. As each member shared a little about themselves, I started to get uncomfortable. I was quickly feeling like the dumbest person in the room, completely out of my depth and like a fraud. My heart was pounding, my body temperature was rising and my mind was questioning why I was here. I was the only member here who was still in full-time employment, and as a result I was still in the very early stages of starting my journey into entrepreneurship. As for the other members? One of them had co-founded an online meal-kit delivery business and was featured on several TV shows; another had launched an upmarket fashion brand dressing the likes of celebrities in the film and music industry after a successful career in the nightclub business, while another had just published his second book.

Their stories filled me with the energy and courage to rewrite mine; to live a better story. Life isn't about who you were yesterday, but about who you have the potential to be tomorrow and what you are going to do about it today. We all hope to have a great story to tell some day, but few like the work and commitment that it takes to make that happen. However, when you are exposed to an electrifying environment that equips you with invincible optimism and acts as a catalyst towards unstoppable momentum, you can't help but take action. 'A mind that is stretched by a new experience,' noted Oliver Wendell Holmes, Jr, 'can never go back to its old dimensions.'

By the end of the meeting, there was this strange mix of feelings that I was experiencing: on the one hand, a heavy case of imposter syndrome; on the other, I was absolutely awestruck by how electrifying the evening was. I came home so energized that I was up until past midnight, sketching out plans and ideas of how I could achieve what I wanted. The mastermind group catapulted my thinking into the stratosphere and helped me to completely reimagine what was possible for my future. I was immersed in an environment in which my desired behaviour and habits were considered normal:

It was normal for them to wake up early and focus on their most important task first.

It was normal for them to think big, act bold and live with courage.

It was normal for them to welcome challenges with open arms as fuel for their growth.

I don't think we meet people by accident. I believe that during our time here on earth, the people that we meet and have conversations with are meant to cross our path for a reason. It's something that we may not appreciate at the time, because so much of life can only be understood in hindsight.

My energy had been ignited and I was ready to play bigger in everything that I did. In the weeks and months after the final group meeting ended, not only did many of these members become friends, but I made quantum leaps in the development of my businesses. Surrounding yourself with energizers who are ridiculously committed to developing and expressing their genius gives you the fuel to transcend your own limitations and see the world through the more empowering lenses of possibility and abundance. And in the process, you can end up achieving goals that would typically take most people years, in just months.

It's why extraordinary leaders from all walks of life make it a priority to seek out extraordinary coaches, mentors and peers, so that they are surrounded by those who think at a higher level than they do or offer an insightful, alternative perspective. Very often, it's this powerful change of perspective that can have a profound impact on how you behave.

The day after Serena Williams crashed out of the first round of the Roland Garros tennis tournament in 2012, for example, she turned to French tennis coach Patrick Mouratoglou. She was already considered one of the greatest tennis players of all time, but she hadn't won a major tournament in two years and her goal was to win one final Grand Slam tournament before retiring.

During their first practice together, she asked Mouratoglou for his feedback, to which he responded by saying, 'First of all, I think you are an underachiever. Yes, you won thirteen Grand Slam titles which is fantastic. But maybe you could have won twenty-six. I say this because I have seen you go to tournaments unprepared many times. I feel like you don't have any plan B when things go wrong. I think you lose too many matches.'

It wasn't what she expected to hear. Here was someone who believed that she had more to give – that she had more than one final Grand Slam win inside of her. The partnership they formed became nothing short of transformational for Williams. Not only did she return to her best form, but she also comfortably exceeded it and went on to win ten more Grand Slams and two Olympic medals. If you want to energize your life, you must electrify your environment and protect it from negative influences.

Design an environment around you that makes it impossible not to succeed

If you want to succeed in any area of your life, you must design an environment around you that makes it impossible not to succeed. The better you get at doing so, the more energy you will have to channel towards that which matters most. And the people that you spend the most time with are just one part of this. Your environment also includes some of the following: what you watch, what you read, how organized the space that you live and work in is, what you listen to, the culture of the organization that you work at and who you follow on social media. You want to be centred in an energetic field that nourishes you and allows you to fulfil your potential.

Here are six ways that you can start electrifying your environment immediately to help you make faster progress to where you'd like to be.

1. Curate your own MBA (Mental Board of Advisers)

Bringing together an imaginary boardroom of advisers comprised of those people who inspire you in some way, dead or alive, is something I did early on before I had the opportunity to meet people who were where I wanted to be in real life, and it is something I still draw upon today.

Select no more than three to five individuals, ensuring that there is as much diversity as possible and that they exhibit the traits that you want to possess. When their counsel is needed – from facing challenges to making big decisions – close your eyes, take a seat at the table and share your thoughts with these carefully selected advisers of yours. Listen intently to what each has to say as you take a mental note of their words of wisdom.

Draw on their perspectives, their energy and their experience; treat their advice as ingredients for the creation of your own recipe and philosophy for success. You may want to change the composition of this board depending on the questions you want help with and as you evolve to that next level of your life.

While the make-up of my MBA has regularly changed since I first started embracing this idea, three individuals have remained in their seats throughout:

- Bruce Lee: for his depth of wisdom born out of his love for philosophy. While I first came across him through his martial arts films, it was his philosophical writings that I connected with most. He was diligent in his journalling and possessed an ability to express this thinking in ways that could be understood by all.
- Sara Blakely: for her extraordinary grit and relentless energy in the pursuit of her dream. She went from door-to-door selling of fax machines to being a sales trainer, and from performing stand-up comedy at night to becoming the world's youngest self-made female billionaire through the launch of her company Spanx.
- Tim Ferriss: for challenging conventional thinking by constantly experimenting with life. His presence on my MBA has helped me to approach life as a series of experiments, opening me up to have the courage to try new things. Rather than focusing on a particular outcome, I get inspired to focus my energy on the wonder of the unknown.

Who would you choose to have on yours?

2. Test-drive your vision board

You may have already come across the activity of putting together a vision board, but have you explored the impact that a real-life vision board can have on your energetic state?

It's an idea that began to form in my mind following the mastermind group experience at the Ritz in London. For the price of a cup of tea and a small bite to eat, I had the opportunity to immerse my senses in inspiration and possibilities. 'Instead of just having a vision board up on my wall, what if I could begin living some of that now in small doses,' I thought to myself. 'Imagine what that could do for my energetic state.' Early on in my coaching career, before I could afford to rent office space and meeting rooms, I would host my meetings at some of London's most luxurious hotels. If it raised my energetic frequency, then I had no doubt that it would have a similar effect for my clients.

Inspired by this, a client of mine decided to have fun with his real-life vision board. He has a vision of living in front of the ocean; so, on a holiday trip to Bali with his girlfriend, he rented out a villa in front of the ocean for a few days instead of staying at a hotel. He has a vision of driving a Tesla car; so he went to book himself in for a test drive to feel what it's like to be the driver of one. He has a vision of making a big difference in society; so he is regularly involved in local volunteering projects. These activities have contributed to raising the energy of the environment around him and, as a result, the belief that his bold vision is achievable.

How can you have some fun in bringing your vision board to life in small ways so you can feel what it would be like to live it?

3. Build your tribe with diversity in mind

Want to live a healthier lifestyle? Join a class or community of fitness enthusiasts.

Want to be happier? Switch off the news and spend more

time speaking with people who are good for your mental health.

Want to progress up the ladder in your industry? Reach out to mentors who have walked the path ahead of you.

Seek out people, groups and communities that remind you of what you're working towards and who are aligned with your vision. The accessibility of social media platforms means that this has never been easier for us to do.

Regularly connecting with new people to expand your network exposes you to more opportunities and inspiring stories. And because we become like the people that we interact with the most, it's inevitable that these experiences will have an impact on your life. When building your tribe, make sure that there is also diversity built into it – diversity in terms of gender, background, experiences, skillsets and expertise.

A conversation with a single parent can teach you about efficiency.

A conversation with a musician can teach you about creativity.

A conversation with a writer can teach you about marketing.

Most of us live in a bubble of people who think like us and work in a similar industry. A diverse environment, however, will energize your thinking because of the perspectives that your mind will be exposed to.

4. Pump some ion

Do you notice a significant change in your energy when you're relaxing on the beach, exploring nature, climbing a mountain, caught in a thunderstorm or walking next to a river?

That's because environments such as these are full of

negative ions – molecules charged with electricity, which serve to energize you as soon as they hit your bloodstream. Charged ions can be positive or negative and occur naturally in the air around you. Without regular exposure to the latter, however, your energy can be negatively affected and that is why doctors may often prescribe that their patients get some fresh air outside in green spaces to improve their wellbeing.

The message here is simple: get up off your chair, go outside your home or office and spend more time outside in nature. It's the one place where an abundance of something negative can be good for you.

5. Cancel your subscription to clutter

In a world of messy maximalism, dizzying complexity and chaotic clutter, adopting a minimalist lifestyle can help you to focus and feel energized. Mess, after all, creates stress by hijacking your ability to focus.

During an interview that I did with Fumio Sasaki (Japan's most famous minimalist and author of *Goodbye, Things*), he shared that after giving away 95% of his belongings, he was able to live with more energy. He was no longer a slave to his possessions. His self-esteem skyrocketed and his apartment felt like a sacred place, almost like a temple. 'When you practise minimalism,' Sasaki shared, 'it's more than an exercise in tidying up. It's an exercise in learning about true happiness. You become aware that you already have everything that you need.' Minimalism is about finding happiness without things.

When you cancel your subscription to clutter within your physical, digital and mental environments, you let go of energy that no longer serves you and make space for fresh energy to flow smoothly in and around you.

6. Change your tune

Music affects your vibration through its power to shift your energetic state to a higher level, and is one of the fastest ways to electrify your environment.

With a total of twenty-eight medals, Michael Phelps is the most successful and most decorated Olympian of all time, and during his competitive swimming career he was known for his ritual of walking out to race in the pool with his headphones on until the last possible moment. The tunes were selected for their ability to calm, inspire and energize him.

What tunes would your playlist consist of, that would have an immediate impact on your mood right now?

Activate the power of love energy

In the outpouring of remembrances following Ruth Bader Ginsburg's death, it became increasingly clear that her husband Marty was her not-so-secret weapon; that she may never have been able to reach her iconic potential had she not had a partner who ranked her career as equal to his own. The Ginsburgs had a partnership built on the foundations of equality.

When you look back at their life together, it's easily understandable why she often talked about her meeting with Marty being, by far, the most fortunate thing that ever happened to her.

After he was diagnosed with testicular cancer, she attended his classes and typed up his notes before getting to her own coursework. Together with their daughter Jane, she followed Marty to New York when he received a job offer at a law firm after graduation. It meant that Ruth had to forgo her final year at Harvard Law School and instead complete her degree at Columbia University. What's important to note, however, is that it wasn't just Ruth making all the sacrifices for their marriage. Marty also played his part. He took on the domestic task of cooking for the family, with their daughter Jane noting: 'Cooking for Mother even when he could not himself eat, nor stand in the kitchen without pain, because for him it was ever a joy to discuss the law over dinner with Mother while ensuring that she ate well and with pleasure.'

And after she got the nomination to the Supreme Court under President Bill Clinton, she said of her husband, 'I have been aided by my life's partner, Marty D. Ginsburg, who has been, since our teenage years, my best friend and biggest booster.' He made it his mission to secure her nomination to the Supreme Court and was her campaign manager. Her success was just as important as his own. In fact, in a study led by Joshua Jackson (Associate Professor of Psychological and Brain Sciences) at Washington University in St Louis that was based on a five-year study of nearly 5,000 married people, it concluded that a spouse's personality has a significant influence on your career success. The relationship that you have at home impacts how you show up in every area of your life, especially your career.

Shortly before his death in 2010, Marty wrote a letter addressed to his wife and left it in the drawer next to his hospital bed. It read:

> My dearest Ruth, you are the only person I have loved in my life, setting aside, a bit, parents and kids and their kids, and I have admired and loved you almost since the day we first met at Cornell some 56 years ago. What a treat it has been to

watch you progress to the very top of the legal world. I will be in Johns Hopkins Medical Center until Friday, June 25, I believe, and between then and now, I shall think hard on my remaining health and life and consider, on balance, the time has come for me to tough it out or to take leave of life, because the loss of quality now simply overwhelms. I hope you will support where I come out, but I understand you may not. I will not love you any less.

Their relationship demonstrated what can be achieved with a strong partnership built on trust, respect and love. Their success is also a powerful example of the fact that you rarely get to the top alone: the bigger, the bolder and the more breathtaking your vision is, the more important the team will be. In a seventy-five-year study conducted by researchers from Harvard University, they found that relationships are the strongest factor in a life of happiness and good health. Robert Waldinger, Director of the Harvard Study of Adult Development, wrote that, 'The clearest message that we get from this 75-year study is this: Good relationships keep us happier and healthier. Period.' This includes LGBTQ+ relationships and the make-up of your inner circle of friends.

When we think about our environment and the role that it has in shaping our behaviour, I believe that one of the partnerships that is often overlooked is that forged between two individuals in a loving relationship. I'm often asked about the people who have contributed to who I am today, and while there are many, there is one that I always mention first: my wife, Laurie.

We first met in my final year of university and spent six months as good friends before we started dating. Ironically, our paths would never have crossed if I hadn't failed my second year. I remember Monday lunch being a favourite moment of mine – the time that we spent getting to know each other over a simple sandwich and bag of crisps would extend so far into the afternoon that I would be sprinting to make my final class of the day. Hours felt like mere minutes and I didn't want it to end. We have gone through a lot together since, and it's her presence in my life that drives me on each day to be a better husband, father and human. She believes in me and is constantly reminding me of my purpose, potential and power. Love, it seems, is one of the most powerful energetic forces there is in this universe. Remember how you felt when you first fell in love and what you found the energy to do because of it.

We're far from perfect; we have our arguments, and we don't always agree on how things should be done. But because we value each other's opinion and champion each other's growth and success, we have developed a formidable partnership in which we feel we can take on whatever challenges arise together. As the author Ryan Holiday summed up nicely in the title of one of his online blog posts: 'The Perfect Spouse is the Best Life Hack No One Told You About'. We are each other's greatest supporter, and knowing this is often all we need to go out and make things happen. My success is our success; her success is our success. The characteristics that form the basis for all successful partnerships – be that in life, business or sport – are these: trust, support and appreciation. When you feel trusted, supported and appreciated by your spouse, your co-founder, or your manager, you show up differently. You show up with more energy and courage to achieve more.

A research study conducted by Carnegie Mellon University psychologists found that supportive and encouraging spouses were a core component to individual success. The team worked with 163 married couples, giving one member of each couple the choice of solving a simple puzzle or taking on an opportunity to compete for a prize. They then recorded the couples' interactions, noting what they said to each other. Those with more encouraging partners were more likely to compete for the prize, while those with discouraging partners who were more critical chose the simple puzzle.

'Significant others can help you thrive through embracing life opportunities,' said Brooke Feeney, lead author on the study. 'Or they can hinder your ability to thrive by making it less likely that you'll pursue opportunities for growth.' When the team followed up with the couples six months later, those who competed for the prize in the more challenging task 'reported having more personal growth, happiness, psychological wellbeing and better relationships than those who didn't'. It seems that supportiveness and encouragement not only make for healthier relationships and happier people, but also shift your energy to focus on possibilities over limitations. You are challenged to become a better person and to use obstacles as fuel for your growth. The power of spending quality time with those that you care about and who care about you must therefore never be underestimated.

When we look at successful relationships of all types, it's our energetic state that influences the quality of these – the energy that you project on to others will be the same energy that they'll return to you. It's the law of vibration in action. When your energetic state is flowing with love, happiness and abundance, you will attract people and experiences that match this. When your energetic state is blocked by fear, doubt and scarcity, you will attract people and experiences that match this. To elevate the quality of our relationships, therefore, we must transform our energy, and that begins with cultivating love from within and embracing the wholeness of your being. As Dr David Hawkins wrote in his book *Healing and Recovery*, 'Choosing to become a loving person results in the release of endorphins by the brain which has a profound effect on the body's health and happiness.' Instead of trying to change people who don't want to change, focus your energy on yourself. When you stop waiting to be chosen and decide to choose yourself instead, beautiful things happen. The right people, opportunities and experiences start to show up, and your energy will be infectious. People will take notice and so will you.

The *New York Times* bestselling author of *Never Eat Alone* and *Who's Got Your Back*, Keith Ferrazzi, said during an interview I did with him that, 'Relationships are crucial to your success, no matter what you want to achieve in your life. They are the lifeblood of our happiness and success. And the most successful are driven by generosity – being of service to others – and not keeping score. Helping others must be something you want to do in order to make the people around you better. Dale Carnegie summed this up well: "You can be more successful in two months by becoming really interested in other people's success than you can in two years by trying to get other people interested in your own success." Do you think a marriage, partnership or friendship will last long if everyone is always keeping score? Not at all.'

Ferrazzi added: 'If you create an environment around you that invites people in so that they can experience your energy and authenticity, you will have extraordinary success. You must first, however, be the kind of person that people want to be around and spend time with. Being the father of a foster son for example, I will spend time with those who want to improve the foster care system. Who want to put some time and money into something that carries meaning to me.'

We are social animals and, as a result, it's important to nourish our relationships – with ourselves, loved ones and others. When you show love to yourself and the people that you care about, you will feel surrounded by the presence of love energy. Not just in your relationships but in every aspect of your life.

9
Get Money to Work for You

'It's not how much money you make, but how much money you keep, how hard it works for you, and how many generations you keep it for.'

ROBERT KIYOSAKI

Dean was an executive client of mine who appeared rich on the outside: a six-figure salary and in a prestigious position at the company that he worked for. He lived in a beautiful home, which he was renting, and dined in some of the finest restaurants that London had to offer. The reality, however, was very different.

Nearly all his income was spent on purchasing things to support an image that he felt pressured to keep up with, and as a result he was tied into his job and the salary he received from it. Each time his salary increased, so did his spending. It appeared that the more he earned, the quicker he found ways of spending it on things he didn't really need. He had got himself into a situation that was preventing him from pursuing what he really wanted to in life, and unless his relationship with money improved, he would never be able to experience true financial freedom and move away from working for money to money working for him.

The value of money is in its ability to be a source of energy: to give you the time to work on whatever it is you want or the ability to wake up each morning without worrying about whether your bank balance will be impacted by the uncertainties of life. The anxiety that comes from a lack of financial security can drain your energy. When you master the flow of money, however, you sleep better at night knowing that the dollars you own are hard at work multiplying themselves into more dollars for you. You are channelling the energy of money into abundance by matching the vibration of that which you desire. While interviewing over 500 millionaires to understand their habits for *The Millionaire Next Door*, the authors Thomas J. Stanley and William D. Danko found most millionaires to be extremely careful with how they managed their finances. They avoided spending much on luxury items, choosing instead to invest their savings in assets that would grow their net worth.

When you spend money to show people how much money you have, you will very quickly find yourself having less money than you'd like. What you come to appreciate as you get wiser is that people are less impressed by what you own and more impressed by what you have accomplished, because it's the latter of the two that inspires. Most people dream about having a lot of money in their possession yet are unable to hold on to it when it does arrive. How can you manage $10,000 a month if you can't even manage $1,000 a month? Unless you have a solid foundation in place, then more isn't going to make things better because money simply makes you more of what you already are. Getting rich and staying rich are two different skills. Just think of all the stories you have heard about celebrities within the world of sport, film and music who have lost fortunes almost overnight. They simply couldn't handle large sums of money. Financial wealth is less about how much you earn and more about how much you get to keep after you have accounted for everything that you have spent your money on. Instead of paying ourselves first, it seems that many of us are paying ourselves last.

When I asked Dean what financial plans he had in place for his future, it appeared that there were none, and it showed when he shared that he had no clue where all his money was being spent each month. He was avoiding the issue and expecting it to just take care of itself. 'Avoidance,' I told him, 'may lead to short-term happiness but it will lead to long-term suffering.' Can you imagine pitching your business idea to a group of investors and being clueless about your numbers when interrogated? You certainly wouldn't get very far. To transform his energy, I got him to start seeing himself as the CEO of Dean Inc. and as a growth stock instead of a stock that nobody wanted to own in their portfolio. It's how the truly rich see themselves and, by doing so, they are careful about protecting and growing their wealth. To start acting like the CEO of your life and demonstrate that you are a stock well worth investing in, you must first address the following:

1. Determine what your current net worth is today. Make a list of all the assets that you own and the estimated value of each: cash in your bank accounts, value of your investment portfolio, market value of

your home and the money you would receive from selling assets such as your car and personal possessions. Then make a list of all the liabilities and outstanding balances that you owe: mortgages, loans and credit card debt. Deduct the sum of your liabilities from the sum of your assets to arrive at your net worth. Write this figure down and update it regularly so that you are always aware of your net worth. If you don't know how much your stock is worth, how do you expect anyone else to? And as your net worth number grows, so will your energy.

2. Make a list of all your expenses in a typical month: bills, subscriptions, dining out, shopping and entertainment. Conduct a cost-cutting exercise by reviewing which of these can be cut or reduced, and start tracking your expenses so that you're aware of where your money is being spent. You want to be in a position where you're living with frugality and have money to regularly save and invest each month. Frugality is fundamental to effective wealth building, and if you're working towards paying off debt, then this trait will help you free up funds to achieve this.

3. Just like businesses must manage their finances to a budget in order to operate efficiently, so can you. Decide your split between needs (expenses that are necessities, such as mortgage/rent, insurance and groceries), wants (non-essential expenses) and savings/investments. While the 50/30/20 rule (50% on needs, 30% on wants and 20% on savings/investments) is often recommended by financial advisers, each of our circumstances will be different. As a parent, my needs will have a higher weighting;

given my lifestyle, my wants will be significantly lower; and my savings/investments will make up the difference. Whatever your savings/investments weighting is, you don't want it to be lower than 10% if you're committed to growing your wealth.

Over the course of the next calendar month, I got Dean to track his spending – if it left his account, it got recorded. When we reviewed what he shared with me, he was able to reflect on what he could eliminate immediately and which of the items added value to his life. It helped him to take back control of his finances – from the monthly subscriptions he no longer needed to the unnecessary expenses that ate away at his income. He also made a list of any outstanding debts that had to be paid off and we gamified the process of him crossing these off one by one.

From here, we then explored building a system that would promote financial discipline and that prioritized paying himself first. When you're able to plan around a budget and know how much you want to save and invest each month to take advantage of the compound effect, you can automate this process so that you don't waste precious energy deciding how you want to allocate your money. Developing a sound financial plan not only improves your relationship and confidence with money but contributes to thinking creatively about ways to make more. Dean has since transformed his financial health: a diversified investment portfolio, a more minimalist lifestyle and a budget that better reflects his priorities have resulted in him viewing his finances as a source of energy instead of a source of anxiety. He is also now in a stronger position to navigate the uncertainties that life will inevitably throw his way – from emergency expenses to unexpected events.

Think rich, get rich

During a one-day workshop that I was running for over 100 aspiring entrepreneurs, I did an exercise to help raise their awareness about their current relationship with money and the impact it was having on their lives. The question was simple yet revealing in terms of how they chose to respond to it: 'What comes to mind when you think of rich people?'

As people's hands shot into the air, I stepped off stage and walked into the audience so that I could hear what they wanted to share. And as I did so, I would repeat out loud their answer so that my assistant back up on stage could assign their words into one of two columns that were marked up on a flip chart. In the first column, we had words such as 'human', 'inspiring' and 'successful'. In the other, we had 'lucky', 'selfish' and 'greedy'.

Once I had received a good sample of responses, I returned to the stage and asked the audience to punch their hand in the air if they wanted to be rich and to experience financial freedom. Unsurprisingly, everyone's hand flew up.

'Wait!' I exclaimed.

'If I heard you correctly, and I'm going by what I have up here on the flip chart, there are some of us here that have a negative association with being rich and yet . . . and yet you want to be rich. So what I'm noticing here is a misalignment that must be addressed if you're interested in making serious amounts of money, because you can't be something that you despise or have a negative impression about.

'If we think money is evil, then to have money would mean that we are evil too. How we see money defines our relationship with it, because thoughts lead to feelings and feelings lead to energy. The question we must reflect on is whether your energy is supporting or hurting your earning capacity.'

Money cannot flow to you when you have negative thoughts about it because you are, in effect, putting up an energetic block to it. You are telling the universe that you can't handle more money and that you don't like the idea of having a lot of money. Before you can get money to work hard for you, therefore, you must take responsibility for your financial health. Doing so puts you in a position to welcome more into your life.

You must be comfortable with the idea of enjoying a wealthy life. When I talk about wealth here, I don't mean just financially; I'm also talking about being wealthy in terms of your health and having the freedom to do what you want when you want through your ability to buy back time. You must be able to visualize and feel yourself living in abundance and enjoying financial freedom, otherwise you simply won't have the energetic force required to make it happen. The role that money plays is that of a key – a key that unlocks that much-desired door to financial freedom. It's why a healthy relationship with money is an absolute must. Treat it as scarce and it will sprint away from you. Treat it as abundant and it will jump into your arms. You must decide the role that money plays in your life.

Don't underestimate just how much of an influence your relationship with money has on your energy. Money is a resource that will help bring your vision to life through its ability to act as a source of energy, or cause you endless misery through its ability to drain your energy. The bottom line is that it's very difficult to lead a successful life if you have a poor relationship with money.

Improving your relationship with money requires you to address your attitude towards it and embrace strategies that can help you turn it into a source of energy. When you're not living from paycheque to paycheque or experiencing financial stress, you have the mental energy required to focus on what matters most. Without some level of financial security, however, your energy is easily drained by all the anxiety. It's important to understand what your current relationship with it is like, therefore, and the following three questions will help you to do so:

1. What feelings come to mind when you think about money?
2. How has your relationship with money impacted your life?
3. What do you feel has influenced your thoughts about and relationship with money?

When I did this exercise for the first time, it was eye-opening in what I was able to learn about myself. Because I never felt like I had enough, I was making decisions based on the choice that would make me the most money – I believed that the more I could make, the happier I would be. It's what led me to choose a career in the financial services industry when deciding what path to pursue in life. As I developed a better relationship with money, my fascination with it increased and as a result I started to do the following:

- Made sure that the composition of my MBA included financially successful people so that I could seek their wisdom when needed to make better financial choices. Their presence is a constant reminder that money is the reward for the value that we bring into the marketplace and that when we receive money, we must not only be grateful for it but take care of it as well as we do the other relationships in our lives.

- Questioned my money beliefs and learnt how those who were able to disprove these successfully did so. For example, I used to believe that you had to slave away for years to earn a decent income until I came across a story of how Alex Tew raised over $1 million in under five months to fund his university education. He did so by building a website consisting of a million pixels arranged in a 1,000 × 1,000 pixel grid and then sold each pixel for $1 to those who wanted to advertise on it.

- Explored how I could increase my earning capacity doing what I wanted, create multiple income streams and develop my knowledge about investments so that I could have money working for me, even while I was sleeping. If you want to make money with your mind, you must feed it with knowledge.

Our relationship with money isn't something that we think about often, because it can be difficult to admit that we have an unhealthy relationship with it – a relationship that can often be heavily influenced by the money mindset of your family, your closest friends and widely accepted norms. However, when you start taking responsibility for it, you begin to adopt more empowering beliefs and create a plan that you can build your financial future around. You can't think about self-care without also giving due consideration to your mindset around money.

From energy spender to energy investor

Dillon Dhanecha is one of those friends who not only embodies the ideas of dreaming big and making an impact in society, but who you can easily spend hours catching up with and that time will feel like only minutes have passed.

Born to refugee parents who moved to the UK from Uganda after being expelled from the country under the dictatorship of Idi Amin, he grew up on a council housing estate with the ambition of making a difference in the lives of those less fortunate, starting at the age of just six years old. Watching the Live Aid benefit concert on TV in 1985 opened his eyes to the horrific conditions faced by so many during the Ethiopian famine. It inspired him to write a letter to Santa asking him to send all the Christmas presents on his wish list to the children of struggling families in Ethiopia – a gesture of such generosity that it got him featured in his local newspaper.

At twenty-four years old he was again featured in the press but this time on the front page of the *Independent on Sunday*'s Money Section, as an online trader making huge profits during the dot-com crash. And since his TEDx Talk in 2010, where he shared an economic model that had the potential to lift African nations out of systemic poverty, he has been working relentlessly to ensure that we can all experience money as a high-energy force for good.

We met to discuss attitudes to money and how our relationship with it can have a profound impact on the wealth that we're able to create, how it can keep us living from paycheque to paycheque or energize us to take risks and be more resourceful in monetizing our knowledge and skills. And we explored the idea that you can't make a difference without making the money and you can't make the money without making a difference.

He shared with me that at one point he was drowning in £107,000 worth of debt. It was the biggest number in his life at the time and it had a significant influence over the everyday choices that he made.

When I asked him how he successfully managed to turn things around and escalate his wealth to where it stands today, he shared an idea that I absolutely loved. He took that debt figure that was killing his energy, added a zero to the end of it and made this £1,070,000 number his financial goal. In an instant, the debt figure went from being the biggest to the smallest number in his life and now he had something far more magnetic pulling him forward. The number itself wasn't the most important; it was what that number would allow him to do. With greater financial wealth, he would be in a better place to help lift communities out of poverty and educate others on how to experience money as a high-energy force for good.

After all, money is energy – it's like the fuel that is needed to get a car from one place to another. The car in this instance, however, is you, and if you have no idea what your destination is, how will you know how much financial fuel is required and what it will be used for? Knowing why you make money will energize you in everything that you do.

According to the National Endowment for Financial Education, around 70% of people who win a lottery or receive a large windfall go bankrupt within just a few years. It's evidence of a lack of purpose when it comes to handling money, because when we have clarity of purpose, we invest money in such a way as to serve our progress towards it. And the more we have, the more energy we have to make that happen. Money needs direction, otherwise you'll never be able to truly transform your relationship with it.

This is a key difference that I have noticed between those who have been successful in turning money into a source of energy and those who struggle. The former not only have a system in place to promote financial discipline, but know exactly what the money they receive will be used for.

When we think of money as energy, we can categorize people into one of two types: an energy spender or an energy investor. Most of us fall into the first type, which is characterized by exchanging our personal energy for money. The relationship is linear – we are employed to do a job and we get paid for it. And it's the comfort zone for many in the sense that it provides our only source of income. Being an energy spender means that you always have to exchange your personal energy for money, and this is difficult to scale because there is a limit to how much energy you can give without burning out in the process. You are effectively working for money.

To get money to work for you and turn it into a source of energy, you must start acting as an energy investor. This second type is characterized by their ability to reinvest their energy to create more money. They do this by establishing additional sources of income and investing energy into assets that will work for them in generating money, thereby moving from a linear relationship between energy as an input and money as an output to a more exponential one. They are always learning and deepening their knowledge on how to extract the most value from the money they own.

Growing up with the belief that there were only two options available when money landed in my back account – spend or save – meant that I was an energy spender, trading my time for money and tying the amount I could save to the salary I was earning. However, once I had a purpose for handling a greater sum of money, I added a third option into the mix: invest a percentage of my salary into tradeable assets and into setting up additional streams of income. It's an option that few of us are taught growing up, but one that can transform how you see and use money.

I remember that the first share I purchased once I appreciated the power of this third option of investing was in Domino's Pizza. My mindset had shifted from ordering pizza because everyone else around me was doing so to using this observation to invest in their shares instead. A few years later, that small investment generated a handsome return and helped to get me on the property ladder. How can you start acting more like an energy investor and get money working for you?

Dhanecha's experience with money illustrates the impact that our relationship with it can have on our energy, our well-being and our quality of life. A lack of financial discipline not only causes emotional stress but prevents us from making meaningful progress towards our most important goals in life. I've seen money drive people apart, tempt people to go against their values and trap people in careers that are soul-destroying by chaining them to mediocrity. When we have a healthy relationship with money, however, it equips us with the freedom to make choices that are aligned with our values and to focus our energy on unleashing our genius into the world. And by establishing a deeper energetic connection towards abundance over scarcity, you send a message to the universe that you are more than ready to receive.

PROTECT

Design your life by designing your days. Stop prioritizing other people's needs over your own. Progress faster by saying no to the activities that are holding you back. Slow down in order to speed up. Remind yourself that the present is all you have and is where your future is manufactured. Take time to connect with nature. Surround yourself with people who challenge you to level up. Create an environment around you that makes it impossible not to succeed. Remind yourself that you never get to the top alone. Cancel your subscription to clutter. Start acting like the CEO of your life. Master the flow of money and it will be a source of energy.

+

PART 4

Supercharge
Your Impact

10
Keep Your Creative Energy Alive

'Formal education will make you a living. Self-education will make you a fortune.'

JIM ROHN

Let's take a moment to review where we're at. We began this book by exploring the importance of energy and how we can awaken our power through a healthier lifestyle, a deeper understanding about ourselves through the medium of writing, an attitude of gratitude and a clear vision of a future that energizes us in the present to plan for it.

We then dived into the process of rewiring our energetic state to match the vibration of what we want to accomplish in life. We learnt how to break free of the blocks holding us back, use obstacles as fuel for our growth and build momentum as a way of generating more energy to power us towards our goals. We then looked at ways of protecting our personal energy, understanding that to keep our energy and vibration high is to attract a more fulfilled life. Having read this far, you have now given yourself a solid foundation to transform your energy and, as a result, transform your life.

In this final part of the book, you will learn how to super-charge your impact by embracing the life of an eternal student, cultivating your curiosity and reflecting on your legacy. You will be reminded about the importance of living with inten-tion in every area of your life and be inspired by the incredible success stories of those who have benefited from applying these energy-based principles. To begin with, however, let's explore why the eternal-student mindset is key to sustaining your creative energy.

Arriving back in the US from his travels across Europe, Joseph Campbell decided that it was time to pursue his PhD. However, after submitting a number of different proposals to the university faculty, he found himself at odds with them.

Despite being an excellent student, he possessed something that the faculty lacked. In addition to being a voracious reader of books, he had gone out into the real world and beyond the walls and corridors of formal education. By doing so, he had enriched his mind through the many insightful conversations he had had with people from diverse backgrounds and the adventures he would not have otherwise had if he had stayed where he was. These experiences ignited his desire to study the things that were calling out to him. Unfortunately, pro-posal after proposal faced rejection by the faculty, and, with no potential for a breakthrough, he left his graduate studies behind.

The world was going through tough times as he left aca-demia behind him – it was 1929 and the Great Depression had begun to impact the lives of every American. After con-sidering his options and arriving at the conclusion that the traditional paths to success were crumbling, with once safe paths now leading to nowhere, the twenty-five-year-old Campbell took what money he had earned from his involvement in music (he played in a jazz band before dropping out in 1928), purchased the books he would need for his self-directed studies in the field of mythology, and made his way to a farm in upstate New York that had a spare room to rent.

He would spend the next five years engaged in a period of intensive, independent study. In his book *The Hero's Journey: Joseph Campbell on His Life and Work*, he states: 'I would divide the day into four four-hour periods, of which I would be reading in three of the four-hour periods, and free one of them . . . I would get nine hours of sheer reading done a day. And this went on for five years straight.'

Upon emerging from his five-year exile of self-study and learning, he was presented with an offer to teach mythology at Sarah Lawrence College, where he remained for nearly forty years. The rigorous self-education that he undertook in expanding his mind allowed him to gain mastery over the subjects and things that interested him. And, as a result, he was able to achieve what he desired: a home where he could continue to be immersed in doing his research, teach his learnings to others who also shared in his curiosities and get paid for it.

He began to write and publish books as a way of sharing his love of mythology and one of them in particular – *Myths to Live By* – would go on to inspire the entire outline for a space fantasy film that a young film director was working on. This young director was George Lucas and, after reading Campbell's book, he immediately went to work to apply everything he had learnt into his film's screenplay. He focused it on the hero as a means of exploring culture, and, with this, the *Star Wars* franchise was born.

Never stop learning

Since quality input always leads to quality output, the nutrition that you feed your mind is just as important as that which you feed your body. If you were to look at my calendar and financial budgeting system, you would observe that a lot of my time and money goes into self-education and for good reason: learning is a habit that energizes you to try something new, opens your mind to new perspectives and inspires you to take action. It's like a workout for the mind, sharpening your knowledge and keeping your creative energy alive. Every time you learn something new, your brain evolves as new connections and thought patterns are formed.

The co-founder of Nike, Phil Knight, reveres his library so much that when in it, you must remove your shoes and bow. It appears that leaders are readers – they continue to expand their knowledge despite what they already know or have accomplished. As you get wiser, you come to appreciate that investing in yourself always pays off – you can't expect to accomplish your big goals if you are playing small in life.

Be a learning machine.

Adopt that white belt mentality.

And embrace the life of an eternal student.

That book you read, podcast you listen to, mentor you learn from, seminar you attend, video you watch or course you take can challenge your thinking and change the course of your life forever. While we are spoilt with the abundance of information available to us, what's scarce is the desire to learn. To learn is to admit that there are people out there who know more than you and so requires some level of humility.

The process of learning gives you options, and, the more options you have, the more freedom you will experience. It is the fuel that enables you to live the life of your dreams. My friend Kylie Flavell, for example, is one of the most inspiring people that I know and is very resourceful when it comes to learning. Arriving in Rome from Australia to live her *dolce vita*, she set out to learn Italian by immersing herself in the culture and living among the locals. Her ambition was to launch her own independent production company, but, without enough money, she couldn't attend film school. Instead, she went on to YouTube and taught herself how to capture high-quality content and use video-editing software. She was also able to tap into online communities of filmmakers who wanted to help each other, and before long she was becoming a one-woman production company – not only is she now able to shoot films, but she is also able to edit, host, produce, market and distribute them.

Within just a few years, this gave her the confidence to negotiate partnership deals with the likes of Samsung, Airbnb, HP and Adobe. And from this came the opportunity to create a stunning collection of high-quality travel videos that took her from the streets and *favelas* of Rio de Janeiro to the markets of Morocco, and from the local villages of Iran to the glitz and glamour of the French Riviera. More recently, she has been learning how to use drones to deliver a more cinematic experience in her videos. During one of our conversations, she shared that, 'We have everything we need to succeed and are only limited by our imagination. If it's your dream and you love it, never stop reaching for it. To do those things that people say are impossible is what truly energizes us.' It's never too late or too early to learn something new because a teachable mindset will always lead you on to the path of progression.

The information that you feed your mind with today plays a significant role in determining who you become tomorrow. You must never underestimate the valuable lessons that you can learn from the experiences of others because success always leaves clues. It can cut your learning curve down by months and even years, but to achieve this, you must be strategic in your approach to learning. And here's how you can start doing so by employing the LARS process, which is all about immersion – the fastest way possible to master a new skill:

1. **Learn.** Reflect on what skills you must develop in order to make significant progress forward from where you are today. When I first started in business, for example, this list included public speaking, marketing and business development. Then decide on how you will go about acquiring this knowledge and when you will schedule time for learning in your calendar. If the vision is important enough for you, you will make time for this in the same way that you always do to watch TV, scroll through social media or check your email.

2. **Apply.** This is an important step and where the real power of learning is, because the value of an idea is only ever realized when action is taken. Learning is meaningless without the opportunity to apply it.

3. **Reflect.** Each time you apply what you have learnt, it's important to take some time to reflect on what went well and what could be improved for the next time. It helps you to avoid making the same mistakes again, and may also make you aware of other skills that need developing that you wouldn't have previously known about.

4. **Share.** The ultimate test of what you think you
   know is in your ability to transfer it to someone else.
   Albert Einstein pointed out: 'If you can't explain it
   simply, you don't understand it well enough.' When
   you must explain what you are learning to others in
   a way that can be easily understood, it helps you to
   carefully organize your thoughts in such a way that
   it deepens your understanding of the material. It
   also holds you accountable for applying what you
   learnt. You could share your learning through a
   social media post, an online newsletter, delivering a
   talk or launching an online course.

We live in an age now where knowledge is so easily acces-
sible and the tools that we need to make things happen have
never been more affordable. What the internet has done is
level the playing field for everyone who has access to a computer and an internet connection. Your ability to use these
resources to deepen your knowledge in new areas and to connect these different strands in innovative ways is one of the
most important skills you can possess in a rapidly changing
world. It equips you with the ability to use obstacles as fuel
for your growth and be comfortable with change. Regardless
of your age, location or educational background, if you
choose to dedicate your life to learning, it will completely
transform your future: your creative energy blossoms and
your desire to constantly experiment heightens.

Eighty-one-year-old Masako Wakamiya decided to learn
how to write code after retiring as a bank clerk. The knowledge that she gained inspired her to design the gaming app
Hinadan, based on a traditional Japanese festival. Since then,
it has had over 100,000 downloads. It would also be the

beginning of a journey that would make her the world's oldest known iPhone app developer and lead to an invitation to stand alongside Apple CEO Tim Cook at the company's annual Worldwide Developers Conference. Now nearly ninety years old, her passion for learning makes her feel more intelligent than ever before and gives her the energy to try more things.

Learning doesn't stop with formal education. It marks the beginning of your real education, for the truly successful person is a student of life. They're constantly stretching their minds, taking on projects that challenge them and pursuing passions that ignite their energy in a way that nothing else can. It keeps them in the feeling of energetic flow. As the futurist Alvin Toffler said, 'The illiterate of the twenty-first century will not be those who cannot read and write, but those who cannot learn, unlearn and relearn.' If you fail to venture beyond the fixed curriculum taught within the four walls of a classroom, you will never realize your full potential and that will weigh on your energy.

A daily commitment to learning can be the difference between becoming a person of influence within your industry and staying in the same position or moving sideways for decades. You set the stage for an expansion in your creative energy, which energizes you to want to learn more, and before you know it, you begin to see an abundance of opportunities raining down around you.

Exercise your curiosity

In an interview with Google founders Sergey Brin and Larry Page, they shared that it was their exposure to Montessori education as children that contributed so much to their independent thinking and success. The Montessori method, established by Dr Maria Montessori at the beginning of the twentieth century, was put forward as an alternative approach to education, with one of its core goals being to build curious children and a love of lifelong learning. Her belief was that building a curious mind allows the child to learn no matter where they go and at any age, as well as discovering their unique strengths and what they enjoy most, because we can never become great at something we don't enjoy. Life is so much more fun when you're able to use your strengths to your advantage. Too many of us, however, waste our energy away on trying to become average at something we hate or are simply not that interested in. This inevitably leads to feelings of frustration.

Instead of simply memorizing facts and following a stand-ardized curriculum, therefore, Montessori-educated children learn how to learn: to ask questions and to find answers. A stronger skill that lasts a lifetime and can lead to personal fulfilment. And the principles that underpin the Montessori philosophy aren't just applicable to children; they can easily be applied and implemented within any type of organization. Leaders who facilitate participation and learning within their teams by acting as catalysts and co-creators create the space for their employees to flourish. Collaboration and experimen-tation are encouraged and, as a result, innovation is born.

Italian chef Massimo Bottura, for example, does this at his three-Michelin-star restaurant, Osteria Francescana, by rewarding novelty over predictability and constantly challeng-ing his staff to look at dishes and ingredients with a fresh perspective. The charismatic Bottura often asks his staff to create dishes based on a piece of music, a painting or a poem. One day, after a moment of inspiration while listening to music in his car, he burst into the kitchen and asked everybody to make a dish based on Lou Reed's song 'Walk on the Wild Side'. After the initial panic turned to excitement, he was presented with a wide variety of dishes – some were inspired by the bass line of the song, some by the lyrics and some by the era that the song was written in. Experiencing novelty in our work and lives, it seems, can unleash our creative energy and broaden our talents.

Curiosity is the energy behind lifelong learning, because you never get bored when you're constantly questioning, exploring and investigating. Life can be an endless journey of discovery and the possibilities infinite, if you have an open enough mindset to explore your curiosities and to allow yourself to wonder. Nearly everything that exists in the world around us – the knowledge that is contained within books to the inventions that make our lives easier – existed first in the minds of the curious. When you operate with a beginner's mind, you create the space and energy for expansion. You come from a place of wonder and openness. You replace fear with curiosity, and you begin to stitch together a more exciting future. Writing for *Harvard Business Review*, Tomas Chamorro-Premuzic shared that curiosity is as important as intelligence. Those with a high CQ (Curiosity Quotient) tend to be invested in continual knowledge acquisition, which gives them a rich toolkit to call upon when crafting simple solutions to complex problems.

A high CQ comes naturally to children who love to ask lots of questions in order to understand the world around them, especially when first exposed to something new. When the investor Edwin Land explained to his daughter that the film he had taken photos on had to be processed, she wondered aloud, 'Why do we have to wait for the picture?' That questioning by his three-year-old daughter would prove to be the inspiration behind the Polaroid instant camera. Children aren't afraid to ask questions. By the time we're adults, however, it becomes a challenge to keep that creative energy alive and as a result our curiosity gets suppressed. To draw out your curiosity, you must ask yourself better questions – a theme we have explored throughout the early parts of this book. The best often begin with the words 'what' or 'how':

- What if it works out?
- What don't I know about you?
- What would make the biggest difference?
- How can I do this better?
- How do I get started?
- How could we be more resourceful?

Following your curiosity doesn't guarantee that what you learn will be useful ahead of time. You just have to trust in the wisdom of your curiosities and that these seemingly unimportant dots will somehow connect in the future. There are dots everywhere waiting for your curiosity to connect them together. As the psychologist and author of *Better Than Perfect* Dr Elizabeth Lombardo says, 'People who regularly seek out fresh experiences tend to be more creative and emotionally resilient than those who are stuck in a very predictable space.' When you have real curiosity and interest in a subject, it never feels like work. And the moment you realize just how little you know is the moment you begin to revive that inner child who is unafraid to ask questions of this world.

You must keep this in mind: nothing is ever finished. We simply evolve and adapt over time. To ask questions and to find answers, just like Montessori-educated children. And to follow that which you are most curious about can often be the very thing that sets you on the path to fulfilment and living with an abundance of energy. Life is a game of infinite wonders and possibilities, and to keep playing you must keep growing, developing and evolving.

Speak less, listen more

There once lived a wise Japanese Zen master.

People from far and near would visit to seek his wisdom. Many would come with the intention of becoming his students so that they might be enlightened in the way of Zen. Grateful for their interest, he seldom turned any away. One day, a well-known and learned professor who was curious about the philosophy of Zen came by.

'I have come today to ask you to teach me about Zen. Open my mind to enlightenment,' he commanded.

The tone of this professor's voice was one of someone used to getting their own way. Smiling at the professor, the master said that they should discuss the matter over a cup of tea. As the master served his guest, the professor immediately jumped into talking about everything he had heard and read about the master, what he was hoping to learn from him, his own background and his own thoughts about Zen.

The master remained silent as the professor continued speaking.

When the tea reached the top of the cup, the master kept on pouring until it began to spill over the table and on to the professor's clothing. Noticing what was happening, the professor stopped talking about himself and said, 'Stop! Can't you see that the cup is already full?'

Calmly placing the pot of tea to one side, the master turned to the professor as he pointed to his cup, saying, 'Like this cup, you are too full of your own opinions and speculations. So full that nothing more can be added. For you to learn anything new, you must first empty your cup. Come back to me with an empty mind so that there is space inside of you to receive something new.'

This Zen parable highlights the fact that when your mind is full, it's impossible to learn anything new. And this is so often a key difference between a master and a student. A student is too fixated on being a master, whereas the master has cultivated the art of being an eternal student. Emptying your cup first creates this beautiful space for you to receive, to learn and to understand. This is the definition of truly listening to another – emptying our minds of the opinions and assumptions that we can be so quick to speak about. With an empty mind, you are always ready for anything and open to everything.

We all love speaking, but only a few really enjoy listening. When I get invited to deliver a seminar for an organization, a question I often get asked is, 'How can I become a better leader?' The easiest place to start, I tell them, is to listen – listen to understand, not to respond – and to ask for help from the people that you lead. We mistakenly think that leaders should know it all and are there simply to tell others what to do. The most effective leaders, however, aren't afraid to ask for help. They see vulnerability as a strength and leadership about connection. People will only follow you if they feel connected to you – they don't care how much you know, until they know how much you care.

One of the greatest gifts that you can give someone is the feeling that they've been heard, understood and appreciated. It's a win/win scenario really when you think about it – not only does it help you build deeper relationships with others, it also allows you to learn something new. And every conversation that you have with another is an opportunity for you to learn, to provide them with an experience of who you are and to leave them better off than before they met you. The less you talk, the more you can listen, and listening always leads to learning.

Winston Churchill's mother, Jennie Jerome, attended a dinner party in 1874 where she met William Gladstone and Benjamin Disraeli, both of whom were competing in the national election to be Prime Minister of the United Kingdom. Asked by a reporter about her experience and impression of each, she replied, 'When I left the dining room after sitting next to Gladstone, I thought he was the cleverest man in England. But when I sat next to Disraeli, I left feeling that I was the cleverest woman.' It wasn't a surprise to the country at the time when the latter went on to win the election. Prime Minister Benjamin Disraeli had spent the whole evening asking her questions and listening intently to her responses. He gifted her with his presence. And he went on to be also regarded as Queen Victoria's favourite Prime Minister.

Be the best listener in the room, encourage others to talk and listen to understand, not to reply. Silence your distractions so that you may listen with intent. For every person that you meet has a story to tell, a lesson to teach and a dream to share.

11
Live a Life
of Meaning

'If you're going to live, leave a legacy. Make a mark on the world that can't be erased.'

MAYA ANGELOU

When Ludvig Nobel died in a fire during a visit to France on 12 April 1888, the French press confused him with his younger brother Alfred – a famed Swedish entrepreneur who made his fortune through the production of dynamite and ballistics.

Alfred Nobel therefore had the rare opportunity to witness his legacy while still alive: to read his prematurely published obituary. Unfortunately, the press ran a brutally negative and scathing epitaph under the headline of 'The Merchant of Death is Dead'. As he pored through every word of the article, he felt heartbroken and horrified. Understanding what his current legacy was, he was determined to live a better story and change his destiny, before it was too late.

In 1895, therefore, Alfred made changes to his will. After setting out what he wanted to give his relatives and staff, he requested that the remainder of his wealth be invested into a fund dedicated to the annual distribution of prizes to those who, during the preceding year, had conferred the greatest benefit to mankind.

And so the Nobel prizes were born.

The truth is that you are contributing towards your own legacy every single day, through the actions that you take or don't take. In fact, many of the happiest and most fulfilled people I know have desires attached to a purpose far greater than themselves. They appreciate that the true worth of our lives is not determined by the amount of money sitting in our bank accounts or what we do for ourselves. This stuff dies with you. Instead, the true worth of our lives is determined by how much more we have given to the world than we have taken from it – the number of lives that we have touched through the work that we do. The defining features of a meaningful life are in the connection and contribution to something greater than the self.

Nine months after opening his first London restaurant in 2015 at the age of twenty-four, Merlin Labron-Johnson became the youngest British Michelin Star chef. Within a year, this was followed by the opening of his second restaurant, Clipstone, and then a third at members' club The Conduit shortly after. In 2019 he stepped away from these projects to focus on his most personal project to date – a new restaurant based in Somerset called Osip (based on his middle name), focused on local produce and connecting with the community around him who work with food. What drives him to achieve the success that he has accomplished in such a short space of time is his constant desire to be and do something better. To keep improving. It is what keeps him moving forward in building his own legacy.

What I find most impressive, though, is what he gets up to outside of the restaurant business he operates in.

During an interview I did with Labron-Johnson, he shared some of the projects that he had been working on. The first was his work with refugee camps. He started running fundraising dinners in partnership with big food suppliers, who would help in donating food for him to cook for his guests. The dinners were held in unique places and all money raised was then sent to his friends in the 'Calais Jungle', helping out with different projects there. They would use the funds to buy food and cook it for around 7,000 people a day. In another project, he went to work with Help Refugees, at one point cooking for around 1,000 people a day with a budget of just 35p per person.

The second was his work with the homeless. Working with Food for Soul in London, he cooked three-course meals for the homeless from surplus food. He didn't just do the cooking, though. He would also serve and sit down with them. By doing so, he was able to see the impact of what he was doing: the meals he cooked would often be the highlight of someone's day and, for others, the best meal they had had in months.

His desire to help others through what he does best started when he first moved to London. Shocked at all the poverty that he witnessed, he began to channel his ambition in a different way to most. He wanted to find a way to help people on the other end of the spectrum to those who dined at his restaurants, and what better way to do so than through what he did best: cooking. He realized that we all have the ability to help others less fortunate than ourselves if we really want to, no matter how small the gesture, and that if we want to be seen as a leader, it comes with the responsibility of helping others achieve their version of success. When we do, we make the world that little bit better. We help make the world a better place for our fellow humans.

There is a Chinese proverb that says, 'If you want happiness for an hour, take a nap. If you want happiness for a day, go fishing. If you want happiness for a year, inherit a fortune. If you want happiness for a lifetime, help somebody.' It summarizes the universal principle that when you put your energy into service and contribution, energy will flow back to you in the form of empowerment, motivation and personal fulfilment.

Whatever your circumstances, we all have the ability to create a difference in someone's life. Think about it for a moment. There's always somebody who is worse off than you are.

It's easy to feel like you don't have much to offer, but kindness for example costs you nothing and is something that benefits everyone. And when you make a difference in people's lives or inspire them towards action, you not only impact their lives; you impact the lives of every person that they will come into contact with throughout their lifetime. It's why kindness and inspiration are such contagious qualities. They light a fire within us to live each day with purpose, poise and power. It's an incredible feeling to see the impact you can have on the lives of others, and it's why I get so much joy from the work I get to do.

Take a moment now to consider what you would want your dream obituary to say about the best version of you – the person that you want to be remembered as. Write this down using the following as a guide:

- What kind of life would it say you had led?
- What stories would it share about you to demonstrate how you lived life to the full?

- What values and qualities would it remember you for?
- Whose lives will it say that you touched and inspired through your actions?
- What will those around you say about the life you led?

Once you have done the above, write down on a separate piece of paper your obituary if you were to stay on the path that you are currently on. How would your family, closest friends and ultimately you feel about your life lived?

When I first completed this exercise, it showed me the gap between the life I was currently living and the life I wanted to live. It was powerful – my energy began to shift away from focusing on the career virtues of money and status, and towards the legacy virtues of impact and contribution. You come to appreciate that no matter how much money you have or how many possessions you acquire, we all go to the grave-yard empty-handed. All that will matter is how you lived and the kind of person you were.

It got me reflecting on the question of 'How do I want to be remembered?' and, as I got clearer on this, I began to act more from this place in the present – to make sure that my actions were contributing to my legacy today. So the question to you is: 'How do you want to be remembered?'

A better story awaits

On my way out of the showers at the gym, I hear someone call 'Simon?'

I assume that he is calling out to someone else who is also

named Simon, so I continue making my way towards the lockers where my belongings are stored. As I take off my towel and begin getting changed, that call turns to 'Simon Alexander Ong?'

Now I know that it's me that he is trying to speak to.

'Hi,' I reply as I turn round to face him.

'I'm Donnie. You probably don't remember, but we briefly met a few years ago when you spoke at the company I used to work with. If memory serves me right, you had some tissue stuck up one of your nostrils during the event?'

I'm stunned.

The only event where I had experienced a nosebleed was this one that he was referring to – my first paid public-speaking opportunity.

After confirming his memory with a smile, he continues, 'I wasn't sure what to expect. Honestly, I only went along because a close colleague of mine was also attending. Anyway, I'm glad I did because everything you said completely resonated with me. It spoke to me, and one of the first thoughts I had as soon as you finished, was "Boy – imagine what I could achieve if I had even a fraction of the energy that this guy has!" I knew I had to start changing up my environment, and one of the first things I did was to start following your work on social media.'

He mentions that he has been following my work for years and that it has impacted his life in ways he could never have imagined. Nearly two years after hearing me speak that evening, Donnie left the company he was with to begin a new adventure following a completely different career path. He discovered that the source of his exhaustion came from living a life that wasn't aligned with his most important values, so he made a commitment to change its direction. He went from being a technology analyst inside a large multinational corp-oration to expressing his creativity on canvas through the medium of paint.

The decision he made, which revealed to him the path that he would have to step on to, was him allowing his inner com-pass and energy to guide him. We all have it, and it's why we worked on understanding what matters most to you in the very first part of this book. A legacy can only be left when you are focused on doing well in the things that matter, and this begins with working on your personal energy.

Before I leave, Donnie tells me that he would love to help me in any way he can as a way of expressing his gratitude for the impact I have had on his life. After I reminded him that it was he who ultimately took action in applying what he had learnt, he suggested introducing me to someone whose rela-tionship would be mutually beneficial. That relationship opened me up to opportunities that I would otherwise not have had, and the experience with him reminded me of a conversation that I had had with a friend who has been a teacher for over a decade. She loves her work and told me that what gets her up in the morning is the knowledge that 'One inspired teacher can positively change a student's life forever. From helping them to overcome what's holding them back to raising their confidence and encouraging them to share their gifts with the world.'

I felt like I had accomplished this with Donnie, but more importantly, I realized that we all have the power to energize others towards a more fulfilling life. When you do something nice for someone else, however small that gesture, you trans-form your energy. And the more energy you have, the more energy you have to give. You don't need to be a professional teacher or even a coach to be an energizer. You simply have to reflect on this question each day: 'How can I add value to someone's life, no matter how small?'

By being of value to others, you bring greater meaning into your existence and in your own unique way will be making this world of ours a better place. As the psychologist Adam Grant wrote in his book *Give and Take*, 'The more I help out, the more successful I become. But I measure success in what it has done for the people around me. That is the real accolade.'

As we near the end of this book, I want to share some important words with you:

You are the greatest project that you will ever get to work on, so make time for pursuing those things that spark a light in you and make you come alive. You will live a better story by doing so. You must be patient, however, because it often takes years before you arrive at that one year that will transform your life forever. You're going to face many challenges ahead, but I promise you that when you understand how to awaken, protect and nurture your personal energy, you will possess the wisdom to unearth the lessons behind every single one of them so that you may come back stronger.

I hope you find the courage to build a life around what matters most to you and follow through with what you know you must do. I hope you listen to that guide within and awaken the hero potential that resides in each and every one of us. I hope you discover the energy to come back stronger and allow your life to flourish in ways that make you want to pinch yourself.

Because one day, when you're old and looking back on life, you're going to wish you had. You're going to wish you had done things differently and you won't be able to travel back in time to change things. But if you commit to making better choices from today, choices that will unlock sources of energy that were in hibernation mode up until now, then you will not only put yourself on the path towards fulfilment, but you will also live a better story and it will be this story that will energize others and become your legacy.

So, you have a choice right now if you want to live a life of meaning: you can either do nothing and continue with how things are, hoping that life will get better, or you can do something about it and surprise yourself by demonstrating what's possible when you ignite that energetic life force inside you. Because being in the beauty of energetic flow is being connected to the truth of who you are and what you can bring into this world.

If you choose the latter, then get ready for the greatest adventure of your life.

It won't be easy, but when you look back and witness your life evolving in the most beautiful of ways, not only will it bring a sense of fulfilment, but that future self will be thankful for the decisions that you chose to make today. Life is meant to be lived, felt and experienced. Don't miss your time while you still have an abundance of it.

Be proud of the person that you are becoming, and imagine what it would feel like not to take one day for granted; not to take your energy and life for granted.

12
Energy is Everything

'The secret of change is to focus all of your energy, not on fighting the old, but on building the new.'

DAN MILLMAN

When Louisa first reached out to me to enquire about my coaching, she was in the process of moving her family to London to begin a new chapter of her life. Having separated from her husband a few years before, she was now a single mum to two teenagers. And to demonstrate her commitment to building a better life for herself and her family, she had sold her highly successful public relations consultancy to give her the mental and physical energy to focus on what mattered most.

For the next chapter of her life, she wanted to take her career and personal life to the next level but was concerned that her private life was sucking all the energy out of her. It's not easy raising children as a single parent. Tougher when you're also having to take care of a brother who is living with Down's syndrome. The result was that she lacked confidence about whether she had what it took to make this next chapter of her life better than the last.

During our first meeting, I wanted to remind her of just how powerful she was. We therefore spent some time reflecting on what she had already accomplished before exploring the exciting path ahead.

'Louisa,' I said as I began to share some of my observations with her. 'You established a successful business with offices in four countries before selling it. Most people are too afraid to take that first step towards even starting their own business.

'You want to focus on something new that will have a positive impact in this world of ours. Most people don't want to be seen to be starting from the bottom again as a beginner in a different industry.

'You have the focus to plan, build and develop businesses while fulfilling your duties as a mum to two wonderful children and a caring sister to your brother. All on your own. Raising children isn't easy and yet you've done this and much more.'

She began to shed some tears as she confessed that she hadn't paused to reflect on her accomplishments in this way before.

'And this is only the beginning,' I told her. 'I believe that you have so much more to offer, and that the universe has so much in store for you.'

During our time together, we addressed her energy leaks, what was blocking her from making the progress that she wanted and how to transform her energetic state. And when I got curious about what that next level of her life looked like, one of the ideas she shared was for a jewellery brand that she had been thinking about while running her public relations consultancy. However, I wanted to dive deeper.

'What else?'

'What else?'

'What else?'

And then she paused.

There was a period of silence – that space where fresh insight and breakthroughs are experienced – before her face lit up.

She said that she wanted to help women step into their power just as she herself had done. She believed that by helping others in such a way, she would also grow, and the idea of this energized her.

To help reshape her environment I invited her to an intimate event so that she could listen to Kristina Karlsson – founder of stationery company kikki.K – and share her journey of turning her passion into a global brand that had stores in over 147 countries. Surrounded by energizers like Karlsson, Louisa was inspired to plan her next moves forward. Inspiration, after all, is an energetic force that breathes life into you, compelling you to take bold action.

What she achieved in the years that followed was incredible to witness.

She was invited to be a keynote speaker at a United Nations conference in Spain.

She launched her jewellery brand, with funds raised from this going towards female empowerment initiatives.

She wrote four short books that are now used as the foundation for many of the workshops and speeches she delivers.

And her private life has gone from sucking all the energy out of her to being a source of energy: she recently became a grandparent to a beautiful boy and is in a relationship with a new partner to share her dreams with. When she speaks about her private life, she now does so in a way that empowers others by touching on how they can cope on their own and still feel love.

The road hasn't been easy. But her children have been a constant reminder of how fantastic life is, and that if you really want to, you can make your wildest dreams a reality. She wanted to show them what's possible. And through her actions and accomplishments, she is demonstrating that, whatever success means to you, it's always a result of how you show up each day and the energy you have to focus on what matters.

Unlock the energy potential in others

'Choose a hand,' I said to Noah. 'If the coin is in that hand, you take the job. If not, you politely decline.'

Noah had just received a strong offer from a competitor to join their company in a senior position that would be a level higher than where he currently was. However, he wasn't sure whether to take it or not, and only had until the end of the week to decide. Staying where he was would provide the most comfort: he was well liked and a valuable member of the team. Accepting the offer would stretch him and he wasn't confident that he could meet expectations.

'This hand,' Noah said as he pointed to my left hand.

'Afraid not,' I replied, showing him that the hand he chose was empty.

Asking him how he felt, he smiled and said, 'I was actually hoping that the coin would be in your left hand. I think I'm excited about the prospect of a new challenge and the new company sounds like an incredible place to be a part of.' This was his energy speaking to him and he was feeling it.

'Tell you what,' I said. 'One more time just to make sure. Go ahead, choose a hand.'

Noah chose my right hand this time and on this try he was successful.

We both laughed at the situation, before I told him, 'I guess you've got an exciting call to make later this week and some bad news to break to your current team. And that coin you're holding? You can keep it as a reminder of this conversation.'

Noah turned the coin over and saw some words etched on the back of it. It was a custom-designed coin that I had ordered, and the message read: 'You have two lives. The second one begins the moment you realize, appreciate and understand that you have only one.' He dropped the coin in his wallet, and, despite going our separate ways once our plane landed in Los Angeles, he told me that he would be in touch again very soon.

Three months later, I received a message from Noah telling me how well he had been settling into his new role and saying that he now wanted coaching with me to help him be the best leader he could be for the team he was now responsible for. While his progress during the time that we have worked together has been beautiful to observe, what has impressed me is how much of an energizer he is in the workplace. As he developed a better understanding of how to manage his own energy, he also started applying these ideas at a broader level.

Noticing the lower levels of energy that his team felt on Monday mornings and Friday afternoons, he decided to get creative. From our partnership together, he knew the effect that our energy has on our wellbeing, behaviour and attitude, and here are some of the things he decided to implement as a result:

- There would be no more team meetings on Mondays, when the team's energy was clearly at its lowest. Instead, these meetings would be held between Tuesday and Thursday afternoons, when the energy was at its highest.
- The team had the option of working from home every Friday, and twice a month on a Friday afternoon there would be events scheduled to promote collaboration, curiosity and creativity. These have so far included inviting guests to speak on an eclectic range of topics – from mindfulness to storytelling and from how to sleep better to developing an entrepreneurial streak in every area of our lives; getting team members to share insights and lessons from activities they do outside of work; and guided wellbeing activities such as yoga and meditation.
- He encouraged the team to switch off from work after leaving the office, on weekends and during holidays. He wants them to be as intentional with their rest as they are with their work and to have the opportunity to recharge properly.

The result is a close-knit team that shows up with more energy each day and who value the environment that Noah has consciously created. His superiors couldn't help but take notice and are now in the process of exploring how they can make these company-wide policies. Noah embodies what it means to be an energizer – somebody who lifts the mood in every room they walk into, who isn't afraid to experiment with their creative energy and who prioritizes time for taking care of their wellbeing.

Be the hero that you have been waiting for

Throughout this book, you have come across stories of clients of mine who have transformed their lives by transforming their energy. They are real-life heroes. And as their guide, the greatest reward for me is seeing them accomplish their bold ambitions and become the person that can make an impact in this world. It energizes me by demonstrating that anything is possible. Hearing the news that my client Emma had made it on to the *Forbes* 30 Under 30 Europe List, for example, sent a huge smile across my face. It was an incredible feeling to see her work being shared with the world and the impact that she was making in her industry.

When Emma first came to me, she had developed her tech business on her own and was now in a position to expand her team in order to grow the business. It presented a new challenge for her, and, having already experienced the power of coaching, she was keen to work together. By the end of our first meeting, it was clear just how much of an impact her personal life was having on how she showed up at work, and as a result, it was the first thing that needed to be addressed.

'I'm always running late to meetings and feeling exhausted, even on weeks when I'm not super busy,' she shared.

'I want to try something fun,' I suggested. 'Imagine that you've just put together your first online course and it's called "Emma's Perfect System for Always Running Late to Meetings and Feeling Exhausted, Even on Weeks That Are Not Super Busy", with me being your first student keen to learn. What would be your seven top tips that would help me to achieve the results you're currently experiencing from using this system?'

While she was unsure of where I was going with this exercise, I encouraged her to play along, and on a piece of paper she wrote the following:

1. Get into arguments with your partner over the most trivial of things.
2. Overschedule your calendar with no room to breathe.
3. Complain about all the things that are out of your control.
4. Spend the free time you do have scrolling through social media.
5. Leave things until the last minute so that you're always rushing.
6. Make money the most important metric for success.
7. Get as little sleep as possible.

'Fantastic! That sounds like the perfect system for those who want to run late for meetings and feel exhausted,' I joked sarcastically.

This exercise helped to elevate her consciousness around all the ways she had been sabotaging her progress and the system that was currently running her life. Emma was able to clearly see how she had been blocking her progress, and, armed with this new information, she now possessed the insights to upgrade her system to one that would deliver better results. Without this level of awareness, we can easily continue blindly on our way without making much progress: busy, but not moving forward in any meaningful way.

By focusing on herself first and taking better care of her

energy, Emma was able to be a more effective leader to herself and others: she hired people who shared the same beliefs as her, empowered them to share their ideas regardless of how crazy they sounded, and crafted an exciting vision that would energize everyone – from the most junior to the most senior – in the organization.

Leaders dictate the energy of the workplace: when they're exhausted, everyone is; when they're full of energy, everyone is.

When I caught up with her following the announcement of her making the *Forbes* list, I asked her what helps to keep her energized through the bigger challenges that she now faces. In her response, she highlighted the importance of visualization and how learning about this from our time together allowed her to be more strategic: 'When I feel down or low on energy, I always ask what the best version of myself would do. It shows me that there is always a way forward and that I already have the answers within me.' Very often, we already know what our next step is; we just have to find the energy and courage to take it. To transcend our limitations so that we may realize our potential.

The stories I've shared in this final chapter about Louisa, Noah and Emma remind us of just how important our energy is to generate any sort of momentum in our lives. When you have big dreams of what you want to accomplish in life, you must make choices that maximize your personal energy, allow you to serve from the best of you instead of what's left of you, and help you to focus your attention on what you love most. If you don't take care of yourself, then who will? When you have the energy to make things happen, anything is possible.

Instead of being frozen in indecision, you act – even when nobody else believes in your vision and everybody is ridiculing you. And that's because . . .

You know that much of success in life is built by consistently doing the work that others aren't willing to do.

You know that taking action builds momentum, provides clarity and creates energy.

You know that when you do what most won't, you will be able to live a life that most can't.

You know that when you transform your energy, you transform your life.

We are energetic beings having a human experience, and energy is the key that unlocks opportunities, the magnet that attracts abundance and the fuel that powers us to extraordinary heights. It's a form of power: what you give energy to, you give life to. Use this precious asset of yours wisely and you will create more of it, and the more energy you have, the more the universe will appear to bend and shift in your favour.

While you can't rewrite your history, you can still change the next chapters of your life. You can release your grip on the pages that no longer serve you so that your energy can flow towards that which makes you feel most alive. Because it's not where you have come from that matters, but where you are going and the person that you are becoming.

And as you begin living in the beauty of energetic flow, you will leave an imprint on this world in your own unique way. You will finally step out of the shadows and into the light to become the hero that you have been waiting for.

SUPERCHARGE

Embrace the life of an eternal student by adopting that white belt mentality. Be a learning machine. Speak less, listen more. Make a difference in someone's life today. Lead with kindness; it costs you nothing and benefits everyone. Give more to the world than you take from it. You already know what your next step is; you just have to find the courage to take it. When you do what most won't, you will be able to live life like most can't. Life is meant to be lived, felt and experienced. It's never too late to begin again and rewrite your story with an ending that gives your life meaning. You are the greatest project you will ever get to work on.

Sources

Introduction: Transform Your Energy, Transform Your Life

Dr Joe Dispenza, *Becoming Supernatural* (Hay House, 2017).

Elly Molina, 'Energy, Frequency and Vibration', Thrive Global, 28 May 2019; https://thriveglobal.com/stories/energy-frequency-and-vibration/.

Ali Sundermier, 'The particle physics of you', *Symmetry*, 11 March 2015; https://www.symmetrymagazine.org/article/the-particle-physics-of-you.

Chapter 1: Invest in Your Health

Brené Brown, *The Gifts of Imperfection* (Vermilion, 2020).

Camille DePutter, 'Mood food: How to fight depression naturally with nutrition', Precision Nutrition; https://www.precisionnutrition.com/how-to-fight-depression-naturally-with-nutrition.

Laura Donnelly, 'Obesity overtakes smoking as the leading cause of four major cancers', *Daily Telegraph*, 3 July 2019; https://www.telegraph.co.uk/news/2019/07/02/obesity-overtakes-smoking-leading-cause-four-major-cancers/.

Barbara Farfan, 'Nike's 11 Maxims and Mission Statement', 9 October 2018; https://www.thebalancesmb.com/nike-mission-statement-and-maxims-4138115.

Craig Lambert, 'Deep into Sleep: While researchers probe sleep's functions, sleep itself is becoming a lost art', *Harvard Magazine*, July–August 2005; https://www.harvardmagazine.com/2005/07/deep-into-sleep.html.

Nelson Mandela, *Long Walk to Freedom* (Abacus, 1995).

Bernardo Moya, 'Weekly Inspirer: 75-Year-Old's Formula for Health, Happiness and Prosperity', *Best You Magazine*, 14 September 2013; https://thebestyoumagazine.co/weekly-inspirer-75-year-olds-formula-for-health-happiness-and-prosperity/.

Timothy W. Puetz et al., 'A randomized controlled trial of the effect of aerobic exercise training on feelings of energy and fatigue in sedentary young adults with persistent fatigue', *Psychotherapy and Psychosomatics*, 14 February 2008; https://pubmed.ncbi.nlm.nih.gov/18277063/.

Sophie Radcliffe; https://www.challengesophie.com/about.

Jasper Rees, 'I've never seen a player lose it with Arsène', *Guardian*, 19 August 2003; https://www.theguardian.com/football/2003/aug/19/sport.biography.

Eva Selhub MD, 'Nutritional psychiatry: Your brain on food', *Harvard Health Blog*, 16 November 2015; https://www.health.harvard.edu/blog/nutritional-psychiatry-your-brain-on-food-201511168626.

David Sharos, 'For 81-year-old body builder, exercise is the key to staying young', *Aurora Beacon-News*, 26 March 2018; https://www.chicagotribune.com/suburbs/aurora-beacon-news/ct-abn-aurora-body-builder-st-0327-20180326-story.html.

Simon Stevens, 'Get serious about obesity or bankrupt the NHS', NHS England, 17 September 2014; https://www.england.nhs.uk/2014/09/serious-about-obesity/.

Tatyana Turner, 'Baltimore bodybuilder, 84, cast in Beyoncé video', *Baltimore Sun*, 8 August 2020; https://www.washingtonpost.com/local/baltimore-bodybuilder-84-cast-in-beyonce-video/2020/08/08/6218870c-d977-11ea-a788-2ce86ce81129_story.html.

Ralph Waldo Emerson, *Journals of Ralph Waldo Emerson, 1820–1872* (Kessinger Publishing, 2010).

Matthew Walker, *Why We Sleep: The New Science of Sleep and Dreams* (Penguin Books, 2018).

Bronnie Ware, *The Top Five Regrets of the Dying: A Life Transformed by the Dearly Departing* (Hay House, 2011).

Mark Zuckerberg, 'Facebook Townhall Q&A', 30 June 2015; https://www.facebook.com/zuck/posts/10102213601037571?comment_id=10102213694974321&reply_comment_id=10102213848471711&total_comments=355&comment_tracking=%7B%22tn%22%3A%22R9%22%7D.

'Obesity linked with higher risk for COVID-19 complications', University of North Carolina, 26 August 2020; https://www.unc.edu/posts/2020/08/26/obesity-linked-with-higher-risk-for-covid-19-complications/.

Chapter 2: Elevate Your Consciousness

Charlotte Alter, 'Sheryl Sandberg Tells UC Berkeley Students What She Learned From Her Husband's Death', *TIME*, 14 May 2016; https://time.com/4336391/sheryl-sandberg-facebook-uc-berkeley-commencement-speech-husband-death/.

Marcus Aurelius, *Meditations*, trans. Martin Hammond (Penguin Classics, 2006).

James Clear, 'Masters of Habit: Rituals, Lessons, and Quotes from Marcus Aurelius'; https://jamesclear.com/marcus-aurelius.

Douglas R. Conant, 'Secrets of positive feedback', *Harvard Business Review*, 16 February 2011; https://hbr.org/2011/02/secrets-of-positive-feedback.

Chanie Gorkin, 'Worst Day Ever?', *Poetry Nation*; https://www.poetrynation.com/poems/worst-day-ever/.

Dr Randy Kamen, 'The Transformative Power of Gratitude', *HuffPost*, 1 June 2015; https://www.huffpost.com/entry/the-transformative-power-_2_b_6982152.

Kira M. Newman, 'How gratitude can transform your workplace', *Greater Good Magazine*, 6 September 2017; https://greatergood.berkeley.edu/article/item/how_gratitude_can_transform_your_workplace.

Marcel Proust, *The Prisoner: In Search of Lost Time, Volume 5*, trans. Carol Clark and Christopher Prendergast (Penguin Books, 2019).

Sonia Rincón, 'Brooklyn Girl Behind Viral "Worst Day Ever" Poem Speaks Exclusively With 1010 WINS', CBS New York, 27 July 2015; https://newyork.cbslocal.com/2015/07/27/worst-day-ever-poem-goes-viral/.

Aram Rasa Taghavi, 'These 7 Bone-Chilling Quotes Will Teach You How to Live Well and Appreciate Life', 13 February 2018; https://medium.com/@ARTaghavi/these-7-bone-chilling-quotes-will-teach-you-how-to-live-well-and-appreciate-life-4e6c40de7d50.

Lao Tzu, *Tao Te Ching*, trans. Stephen Addiss and Stanley Lombardo (Hackett Publishing, 1993).

Robin Wall Kimmerer, 'The Serviceberry: An Economy of Abundance', *Emergence Magazine*, 10 December 2020; https://emergencemagazine.org/essay/the-serviceberry/.

Bronnie Ware, *The Top Five Regrets of the Dying: A Life Transformed by the Dearly Departing* (Hay House, 2011).

William Arthur Ward, *Fountains of Faith* (Droke House, 1970).

Sarah Young, 'Each Day Is a Gift: Woman's Heartbreaking Letter Goes Viral After Her Death at Age 27', *Independent*, 7 January 2018; https://www.independent.co.uk/life-style/holly-butcher-death-27-ewing-s-sarcoma-cancer-viral-letter-facebook-a8146271.html.

'An experiment in gratitude – The science of happiness', SoulPancake, 12 July 2013; https://www.youtube.com/watch?v=oHv6vTKD6lg.

'Southwest Careers', Southwest Airlines; https://careers.southwestair.com/culture.

Chapter 3: Focus on What Matters Most

Charles Chu, 'Bruce Lee achieved all his life goals by his death at age 32 because of one personality trait', *Quartz*, 16 March 2017; https://qz.com/932799/bruce-lee-achieved-all-his-life-goals-by-32-by-committing-to-one-personality-trait/.

Paulo Coelho, *The Alchemist* (HarperCollins, 1995).

Timothy Ferriss, *The 4-Hour Work Week: Escape the 9–5, Live Anywhere and Join the New Rich* (Vermilion, 2011).

Carmine Gallo, 'Conquer public speaking nerves with Carli Lloyd's peak performance secret', *Forbes*, 9 July 2015; https://www.forbes.com/sites/carminegallo/2015/07/09/

conquer-public-speaking-nerves-with-carli-lloyds-peak-performance-secret/?sh=523de10c1a91.

Robert Greene, *Mastery* (Profile Books, 2012).

C. G. Jung, *C. G. Jung Letters, Volume 1: 1906–1950*, ed. Gerhard Adler and Aniela Jaffé, trans. R. F. C. Hull (Princeton University Press, 1973).

John C. Maxwell, *The 15 Invaluable Laws of Growth* (Center Street, 2012).

Mark H. McCormack, *What They Don't Teach You at Harvard Business School* (Profile Books, 2014).

Randy Milgrom, 'Skunk works', *Michigan Engineering*, 27 June 2016; https://medium.com/@UMengineering/skunk-works-2403ed8bf74c.

Nandagopal Rajan, 'Be a source of energy for others: Microsoft CEO Satya Nadella's lesson for the youth of India', *Financial Express*, 1 October 2014; https://www.financialexpress.com/archive/be-a-source-of-energy-for-others-microsoft-ceo-satya-nadellas-lesson-for-the-youth-of-india/1294529/.

Sir Ken Robinson with Lou Aronica, *The Element: How Finding Your Passion Changes Everything* (Penguin Books, 2010).

Sri Swami Satchidananda, *The Yoga Sutras of Patanjali* (Integral Yoga Publications, 2012).

Musa Tariq, 9 February 2018; https://twitter.com/musa/status/962090925978726400.

Chapter 4: Break Free of Your Energetic Blocks

Muhammad Ali with Richard Durham, *The Greatest: My Own Story* (Graymalkin Media, 2015).

Aristotle with commentary by Renford Bambrough, *The Philosophy of Aristotle*, trans. A. E. Wardman (Signet, 2011).

Rob Brezsny, *Pronoia is the Antidote for Paranoia: How the Whole World is Conspiring to Shower You with Blessings* (North Atlantic Books, 2009).

Mayra Cuevas, 'In a superhero cape, he feeds the city's hungry and homeless. And he's only 4', CNN, 25 February 2019; https://edition.cnn.com/2018/05/21/us/iyw-boy-helps-homeless-trnd/index.html.

Raúl de la Fuente-Fernández et al., 'Expectation and dopamine release: Mechanism of the placebo effect in Parkinson's disease', *Science*, 10 August 2001; https://science.sciencemag.org/content/293/5532/1164.

Fred H. Goldner, 'Pronoia', *Social Problems*, 30:1 (1982); https://www.jstor.org/stable/800186.

Benjamin Hardy, 'To Have What You Want, You Must Give Up What's Holding You Back', 9 June 2018; https://medium.com/the-mission/to-have-what-you-want-you-must-give-up-whats-holding-you-back-65275f844a5a.

Sharon Salzberg, 'How to Recognize Your Inner Critic', *Mindful*, 3 May 2018; https://www.mindful.org/how-to-recognize-your-inner-critic/.

Sharon Salzberg, *Real Love: The Art of Mindful Connection* (Macmillan, 2017).

Brianna Wiest, *Ceremony* (Thought Catalog Books, 2021).

Marianne Williamson, *A Return to Love* (Thorsons, 2015).

'An apprentice asks his master . . .', Here Yoga, 21 May 2020; https://www.facebook.com/hereyogastudio/posts/an-apprentice-asks-his-master-when-is-the-best-time-to-plant-a-tree-the-master-r/16788411355996632/.

'Ceregene, Inc. Advances Phase 2b CERE-120 (AAV2-neurturin) Trial in Parkinson's Disease', BioSpace, 3 February 2011; https://www.biospace.com/article/releases/ceregene-inc-advances-phase-2b-cere-120-aav2-neurturin-trial-in-parkinson-s-disease-/.

'Unlocking the healing power of you', *National Geographic*; https://www.nationalgeographic.com/magazine/article/healing-science-belief-placebo.

Chapter 5: Turn Obstacles into a Source of Energy

Steve Anderson, *The Bezos Letters: 14 Principles to Grow Your Business Like Amazon* (Morgan James Publishing, 2019).

Shaunta Grimes, 'It is not the strongest that survives', 24 March 2019; https://medium.com/the-1000-day-mfa/it-is-not-the-strongest-that-survives-973a39f0d026.

Haruki Murakami, *Kafka on the Shore* (Vintage, 2005).

Srinivas Rao, 'A Tolerance for Uncertainty is the Price of Admission for an Extraordinary Life', 10 October 2018; https://medium.com/the-mission/a-tolerance-for-uncertainty-is-the-price-of-admission-for-an-extraordinary-life-a745db742047.

'The best advice I ever got', *Fortune*, 25 October 2012; https://fortune.com/2012/10/25/the-best-advice-i-ever-got/.

Chapter 6: Make Momentum Your Friend

Dale Carnegie Training, *The 5 Essential People Skills* (Simon & Schuster, 2009).

Jonathan Fields, *How to Live a Good Life* (Hay House, 2016).

Regina Kramer, 'Commitment and the Universe: How making a commitment to what I really wanted transformed my entire life', Thrive Global, 4 April 2018; https://thriveglobal.com/stories/commitment-and-the-universe/.

Anaïs Nin, *The Diary of Anaïs Nin, Volume Three, 1939–1944* (Harcourt, Brace & World, 1969).

'Denzel Washington at NAACP Image Awards: Ease is a Greater Threat to Progress than Hardship', *DiversityInc*, 14 February 2017; https://www.diversityinc.com/denzel-washington-naacp-image-awards-ease-greater-threat-progress-hardship/.

'Steve Jobs on Failure', Silicon Valley Historical Association, 31 October 2011; https://www.youtube.com/watch?v=zkTfoLmDqKI.

Chapter 7: Manage Your Energy, Not Your Time

Iwona Blazwick, 'The artist is present', *Art Monthly*, September 2011; https://www.artmonthly.co.uk/magazine/site/article/marina-abramovic-interviewed-by-iwona-blazwick-september-2011.

Catherine Clifford, 'What Warren Buffett taught Bill Gates about managing time by sharing his (nearly) blank calendar', CNBC, 7 September 2018; https://www.cnbc.com/2018/09/07/warren-buffett-taught-bill-gates-about-time-management-by-sharing-his-blank-calendar.html.

Ina Jürgens, '10 Zen Quotes and Proverbs', *Just Breathe Magazine*, 9 December 2014; https://justbreathemag.com/mind/new-consciousness/10-zen-quotes-and-proverbs/.

David L. Kirp, 'Meditation transforms roughest San Francisco schools', 12 January 2014; https://www.sfgate.com/opinion/

openforum/article/Meditation-transforms-roughest-San-Francisco-5136942.php.

Ankesh Kothari, 'The Worst Fisherman That Ever Lived', 22 February 2010; https://www.productiveflourishing.com/the-worst-fisherman-that-ever-lived/.

Laura-Blaise McDowell, 'How J. K. Rowling created the incredible world of Harry Potter', *Bookstr*, 18 June 2018; https://bookstr.com/article/how-j-k-rowling-created-the-incredible-world-of-harry-potter/.

Thich Nhat Hanh, *Touching Peace: Practising the Art of Mindful Living* (Parallax Press, 2005).

Amit Ray with Banani Ray, *World Peace: The Voice of a Mountain Bird* (Inner Light Publishers, 2014).

Allison Rimm, 'Taming the Epic To-Do List', *Harvard Business Review*, 26 March 2018; https://hbr.org/2018/03/taming-the-epic-to-do-list.

Danielle F. Shanahan et al., 'Health Benefits from Nature Experiences Depend on Dose', 23 June 2016; https://www.nature.com/articles/srep28551.

Jeremy A. Smith et al., 'The State of Mindfulness Science: Here's what we know right now about mediation – and what we don't', *Greater Good Magazine*, 5 December 2017; https://greatergood.berkeley.edu/article/item/the_state_of_mindfulness_science.

Colin Turner, *The Teachings of Billionaire Yen Tzu (Volume 1): Infinite Patience, Immediate Results* (21st Century Books, 2004).

Colin Turner, *The Teachings of Billionaire Yen Tzu (Volume 2): Realising Desires, Needing Nothing* (21st Century Books, 2004).

Bertrand Venard, 'The story of Ruth Handler, the creator of Barbie and co-founder of Mattel', *Women's Agenda*, 17 June 2019;

https://womensagenda.com.au/latest/the-story-of-ruth-handler-the-creator-of-barbie-co-founder-of-mattel/.

Rachel Wolchin, *What You Missed While Blinking* (The Good Quote Publishing, 2020).

Chapter 8: Electrify Your Environment

Dale Carnegie, *How to Win Friends and Influence People* (Vermilion, 2006).

James Clear, *Atomic Habits* (Random House Business, 2018).

Gerry Everding, 'Spouse's personality influences career success, study finds', Washington University in St Louis, 18 September 2014; https://source.wustl.edu/2014/09/spouses-personality-influences-career-success-study-finds/.

David Hawkins, *Healing and Recovery* (Veritas Publishing, 2009).

Ryan Holiday, 'The Perfect Spouse Is the Best Life Hack No One Told You About', 21 December 2015; https://ryanholiday.net/the-perfect-spouse-is-the-best-life-hack-no-one-told-you-about/.

Oliver Wendell Holmes, *The Autocrat of the Breakfast Table* (Echo Library, 2006).

Bruce A. Mason, 'How negative ions produce positive vibes', *HuffPost*, 11 December 2017; https://www.huffpost.com/entry/how-negative-ions-produce-positive-vibes_b_5a2eca7fe4b00be52e9d4ae2.

Patrick Monahan, 'Supportive relationships linked to willingness to pursue opportunities', Carnegie Mellon University, 11 August 2017; https://www.cmu.edu/dietrich/news/news-stories/2017/august/supportive-spouses-brooke-feeny.html.

Michelle Ruiz, 'May every woman find her Marty Ginsburg', *Vogue*, 28 September 2020; https://www.vogue.co.uk/arts-and-lifestyle/article/marty-ginsburg.

Robert Waldinger, 'What makes a good life? Lessons from the longest study on happiness', TED, 15 November 2015; https://www.ted.com/talks/robert_waldinger_what_makes_a_good_life_lessons_from_the_longest_study_on_happiness/transcript?language=en#t-388180.

Chapter 9: Get Money to Work for You

Dillon Dhanecha, 'Africa: Inspiring and be inspired', TED, 26 November 2010; https://www.youtube.com/watch?v=jeZiko4SoSc.

Dillon Dhanecha, 'What My First Mentor Taught Me', 22 May 2019; https://www.legacymakers.global/post/what-my-first-mentor-taught-me.

Robert T. Kiyosaki, *Rich Dad Poor Dad* (Plata Publishing, 2017).

George Loewenstein, 'Five myths about the lottery', *Washington Post*, 27 December 2019; https://www.washingtonpost.com/outlook/five-myths/five-myths-about-the-lottery/2019/12/27/742b9662-2664-11ea-ad73-2fd294520e97_story.html.

Thomas J. Stanley and William Danko, *The Millionaire Next Door: The Surprising Secrets of America's Wealthy* (Taylor Trade Publishing, 2010).

Chapter 10: Keep Your Creative Energy Alive

Joseph Campbell, *The Hero's Journey* (New World Library, 2014).

Joseph Campbell with David Kudler and Johnson E. Fairchild, *Myths to Live By* (Joseph Campbell Foundation, 2011).

Tomas Chamorro-Premuzic, 'Curiosity is as important as intelligence', *Harvard Business Review*, 27 August 2014; https://hbr.org/2014/08/curiosity-is-as-important-as-intelligence.

John Coleman, 'For those who want to lead, read', *Harvard Business Review*, 15 August 2012; https://hbr.org/2012/08/for-those-who-want-to-lead-rea.

Burt A. Folkart, 'Obituaries: Joseph Campbell; scholar in mythology', *Los Angeles Times*, 3 November 1987; https://www.latimes.com/archives/la-xpm-1987-11-03-mn-18155-story.html.

Francesca Gino, 'The business case for curiosity', *Harvard Business Review* (Spotlight Series), September–October 2018; https://hbr.org/2018/09/the-business-case-for-curiosity.

Francesca Gino, 'What the world's best restaurant knows about keeping its creative edge', *Harvard Business Review*, 29 June 2018; https://hbr.org/2018/06/what-the-worlds-best-restaurant-knows-about-keeping-its-creative-edge.

Elizabeth Lombardo, *Better than Perfect* (Seal Press, 2014).

Jim Rohn, *The Ultimate Jim Rohn Library* (Nightingale-Conant, 2017).

Alvin Toffler, *Future Shock* (Ballantine Books, 2022).

'Famous Montessori Child: Google and Montessori', Montessori Education; https://www.montessorieducation.com/blog/google-and-montessori.

'The Great Rivalry', Gladstones Library, 24 October 2017; https://www.gladstoneslibrary.org/news/volume/the-great-rivalry-as-told-by-punch.

Chapter 11: Live a Life of Meaning

Maya Angelou, *Maya Angelou: The Complete Poetry* (Virago, 2015).

Maya Angelou, *Pocket Maya Angelou Wisdom* (Hardie Grant Books, 2019).

Sean Braswell, 'The Newspaper Error that Sparked the Nobel Prize', 9 October 2015; https://www.ozy.com/true-and-stories/the-newspaper-error-that-sparked-the-nobel-prize/40007/.

Adam Grant, *Give and Take* (W&N, 2014).

Chapter 12: Energy is Everything

Dan Millman, *Way of the Peaceful Warrior: A Book That Changes Lives* (H. J. Kramer, 2000).

Acknowledgements

This book would not be in your hands if it wasn't for the following people, to whom I am truly grateful:

To the team at Penguin Random House, thank you for taking me on as an author and believing in what I had to offer. To Martina O'Sullivan, thank you for responding to that first message of mine back in 2019 and for your generosity in making the time to meet, listen to my ideas and offer valuable advice as I embarked on this exciting journey. To Lydia Yadi, thank you so much for your incredible support and encouragement throughout. Your input and feedback have been priceless. To Celia Buzuk, thank you for your patience and helpful advice throughout the writing process, which has shaped the book into being the best it can be. You have all challenged me to be the best writer I can be, and I am blessed to have had such a wonderful team to work with in the creation of this book.

To my agent, Kizzy Thomson, thank you for helping me to navigate this journey and for seeing the impact that this project can have on the lives of others. I am also grateful to fellow author and entrepreneur Ash Ali, for introducing me to Kizzy. Thank you for your support, Ash, and for being the incredible inspiration that you are.

To my beautiful wife, Laurie, thank you for always being there for me and being my biggest supporter. It's a blessing to have someone who believes in me the way that you do, and your help throughout the writing process, which coincided with when we became parents for the first time, has been immense. My success is our success, and having you and our daughter Sienna by my side energizes me to be better than who I was yesterday. You are one of the secret ingredients to the progress I have been able to make since we first met at the London School of Economics in 2006.

To my dad, Alex, and his partner, Pat, thank you for the lessons you have taught me over the years – many of which have played an instrumental role in my journey from employee to entrepreneur and to creating a life that allows me to have a positive influence on the lives of others. To my brother Ian and his wife, Rachel, thank you for your help and feedback during the writing of this book despite also becoming parents for the first time.

To Marc Alfred Tidd, thank you for seeing the potential that I had within me and for the invitation to be a part of the mastermind group that you ran. To the energizers of this group – Dominic Knight, Patrick Drake, Marc Burton, Dillon Dhanecha, Gaven Orlando, Kylie Flavell, Ayee Marie McGrath, Massimo Stocchi, Pritan Ambroase, Ahmet Mikko, Mellissa Laycy and Luke Bradford, thank you for challenging me to be better each day and for opening my eyes to a world of possibilities that I never knew existed before. This experience with you helped to shape my thinking and demonstrated the power of an electrifying environment.

To the extraordinary humans who kindly allowed me to interview them and whom I have referenced throughout this book – Sophie Radcliffe, Rhiannon Lambert, Diana Chao, Musa Tariq, Bob Burg, Keith Ferrazzi, Fumio Sasaki and Merlin Labron-Johnson – thank you for your time in sharing your wisdom, insights and stories. They have not only inspired me but I've no doubt that they will also inspire the readers of this book.

To Hasan Kubba, Ali Abdaal, Robin Waite, James Jani, Simon Severino and Sean Wes, thank you for creating the space for me to share my thoughts with you, to ask for help and to learn from you. Your stories are an inspiration to me.

To Bev James and her training team at The Coaching Academy – Kris Robertson, Dave Pill, Sarah Urquhart, Gordon Urquhart, Pam Lidford, Ann Skidmore, Jan Lonnen and Andrew Jenkins – thank you for opening my eyes to the transformative power of coaching and for providing me with the tools to share this with others.

To Jamie Smart – one of the first coaches that I started working with – thank you for helping me to understand the nature of thought, the beauty of connection and the unexpected keys to clarity. The investment in our time together opened my mind to a series of insights that have contributed to the person I am today.

To my coaching clients, thank you for trusting in me to be your guide and for inspiring me through your actions and your courage to be vulnerable in our sessions together. Witnessing your transformation is the reason why I started this journey into the world of coaching and personal development.

To those who have invited me to speak at conferences and company events, thank you for believing in me and for giving me the opportunity to share my insights and stories with your audiences.

To my newsletter subscribers and followers on social media, thank you for your support over the years, especially if you have been there since the beginning of my journey. I am grateful for every like, comment, share and message, and I hope that my posts have had a positive impact on your life in however small a way.

And finally, to you the reader, thank you so much for purchasing a copy of this book. It means more to me than you'll ever know, and I look forward to connecting with you further online over social media or email.

Connect with Simon

simon@simonalexanderong.com

@simonalexandero

@SimonAlexanderO

PENGUIN PARTNERSHIPS

Penguin Partnerships is the Creative Sales and Promotions team at Penguin Random House. We have a long history of working with clients on a wide variety of briefs, specializing in brand promotions, bespoke publishing and retail exclusives, plus corporate, entertainment and media partnerships.

We can respond quickly to briefs and specialize in repurposing books and content for sales promotions, for use as incentives and retail exclusives as well as creating content for new books in collaboration with our partners as part of branded book relationships.

Equally if you'd simply like to buy a bulk quantity of one of our existing books at a special discount, we can help with that too. Our books can make excellent corporate or employee gifts.

Special editions, including personalized covers, excerpts of existing books or books with corporate logos can be created in large quantities for special needs.

We can work within your budget to deliver whatever you want, however you want it.

For more information, please contact
salesenquiries@penguinrandomhouse.co.uk